RETURN TO GREATNESS
DRIVING THE AMERICAN DREAM

CLIFTON LAMBRETH
WITH
MARY CALIA & PATRICK DOYLE

Illustrations by Igor Babailov

D1445010

RETURN TO GREATNESS
DRIVING THE AMERICAN DREAM

CLIFTON LAMBRETH
WITH
MARY CALIA & PATRICK DOYLE

Illustrations by Igor Babailov

Return To Greatness:
DRIVING THE AMERICAN DREAM

Published by Imagine Media Publishing
A division of Imagine Media Solutions, Inc.
741-B Madison Street
Clarksville, TN 37040
(931) 648-1788
Fax: (931) 443-0063
www.imaginemediasolutions.com

ISBN: 978-0-578-04361-6
Printed in the United States of America

www.thereturntogreatness.com

www.thefordbook.com
www.fordbook.com

Illustrations by Igor Babailov
www.babailov.com

Cover Design by David W. Shelton

American flag cover photo: ©iStockPhoto/Liliboas

THIS BOOK IS NEITHER AUTHORIZED NOR SPONSORED BY FORD MOTOR COMPANY.

The Publisher, authors and illustrator, make no claims to rights in any of the trademark for products of Ford Motor Company depicted on the cover and in the illustrations of this book, which are the exclusive property of Ford Motor Company.

CONTENTS

ACKNOWLEDGEMENTS

Thanks to Melissa Webb, for all her efforts on the *Ford and the American Dream* project. A special thanks to my wife, Susan Lambreth, for the incredible amount of time she put into editing and being a perfect accountability partner. Her faith in us and her belief in this project helped make the book a reality.

— *Clifton Lambreth*

"If there was any one secret of success,
it lies in the ability to get the other person's point of view
and see things from that person's angle
as well as from your own."
— Henry Ford

INTRODUCTION

"Do the right thing at the right time with the right motivation
and you will get the right results, but more importantly, you will
earn the right to expect others to do the same."
— Henry Ford

CHRISTOPHER HOPE'S OFFICE within the world headquarters of Ford Motor Company in Dearborn, Michigan, was flooded with the sounds of a hectic workday as usual. Christopher had been with Ford for more than 25 years, and had worked his way up the ladder to his current position as vice-president of public relations. At the helm of communications operations for such a corporate giant, he was used to incessant activity, especially lately.

It had been almost a year now since the 2006 reports had surfaced mentioning threats of bankruptcy facing the Ford Motor Company. The news had just become worse, with announcements of multi-billion dollar losses and thousands of job layoffs. Amazingly, the negative news only seemed to heighten the American public's fascination with Ford and the American automobile industry. With every negative news clip came more and more attention.

For months he had been fielding requests for information, interviews, and the insider scoop from all directions.

Christopher handled each request with practiced proficiency, always looking for the positive that he could weave in amongst the bad reports.

He hoped the old adage — "all press is good press, even the bad" — was really true.

As he always did first thing in the morning, Christopher made his way around the department, checking on his team and making sure everyone was clear on their tasks for the day. It was nearly nine o'clock by the time he finally arrived back at his office, where he could gather his thoughts.

Christopher Hope was born in North Carolina and had been relocated with Ford several times before arriving in Dearborn. He was considered one of the best and brightest MBA graduates from Western Carolina University, where the company had plucked him many years ago. He had been a proud member of the Ford team ever since, and had done well to live up to the promises of his stellar academic career.

An impressively tall man in stature, he did his best to keep in good physical condition, as he believed in the philosophy of sound body and sound mind. His boyish charm and larger-than-life smile would disarm even the most vicious adversary. Christopher exuded quiet strength and optimism. Quick wit combined with sharp analytical abilities served him well in his communications responsibilities. He had an inexhaustible energy for what he felt was his mission in life. Books were his passion — classics, historical novels, biographies, especially wits, wisdom and inspirational leadership — and he shared the lessons he learned with the people around him. He believed in God, prayer, family, community service, and the American Dream.

Seated at his desk, he removed his laptop from his briefcase and checked his email for the second time that day. He always looked through his emails at least once during the morning before leaving home. Usually at least a couple of new messages from international journalists and publications were received during the night. As he glanced through the latest list of incoming messages, one in particular caught his eye. Frank McIntyre, a senior staff reporter for a Detroit paper, had sent a message saying that he would be calling later in the morning to follow up on a conversation they had the day before.

Frank was one of the few reporters Christopher truly trusted. Frank was positive and fair in his reporting, certainly an exception to the unspoken rule that Christopher imagined required reporters to constantly go for the negative. Because of his tendency toward the positive and the truth, he usually made an extra effort to funnel information to Frank for any stories he was working on.

Christopher tapped out a reply to Frank telling him that he would be available to talk with him in the next hour. As he did with all of his emails, he included a quote at the bottom of the message — a quote by Charles Swindoll that aptly summed up Christopher's outlook on life:

"The longer I live, the more important I realize the impact of attitude on life. It is more important than the past, than education, than money, than circumstances, than failures, than successes, than what other people think or say or do. It is more important than appearance, giftedness, or skill. The remarkable thing is we have a choice every day of our lives regarding the attitude we embrace for that day. We cannot change our past. We cannot change the fact that people will act in a certain way. We cannot change the inevitable. The only thing that we can do is play on the one string that we have, and that is our attitude... I'm convinced that life is 10 percent what happens to me, and 90 percent how I react to it. And so it is with you. We are in charge of our attitudes."

Christopher felt a responsibility to share his knowledge and ideas and to try to inspire others. He saw himself as a messenger seeking opportunities to bring good news and make the world a better place. The impossible was always possible and dreams were never too big. Problems didn't exist; they were only growth opportunities. His view of the world stretched to his role in leadership at Ford. He saw the challenges at Ford as opportunities to improve and excel. Perhaps that was why he was always able to find the positive in any situation.

As a veteran of many Ford battles such as the Pinto fuel tank recall, the owner dialogue program, the Firestone fiasco, and the Navistar nightmare, he had gained experience and wisdom along the way. He was battle-tested.

In contrast to his long-standing record of loyalty to Ford, the company's senior leadership had changed drastically over the years. The leadership seemed to transition from car people to big-exec types on the look-out for megabucks, but with no real passion for the automobile business. They were hired guns who, like mercenaries, took what they wanted, then bailed out when the going got tough. Thus the average tenure of top executives had dwindled to five years or less as they jumped to the next ship, much like pirates searching for another ship's treasure to plunder.

The transitional nature of Ford's management had created a fear of being fired or transferred, becoming a victim of the right-of-assignment rule, or forced into an early retirement package. Ford corporate hallways were busy with workers whom, Christopher often found, were frustrated because no one seemed to listen to their voices. Thus, employees rarely communicated with management or each other about what was really on their minds. The Ford environment was becoming less collegial every day.

In late March, 2007, a major storm was brewing at Ford Motor Company. Doomsday, it seemed, loomed on the horizon. The company was about to experience an earthquake that would rock the planet of Ford. Christopher knew that in the summer months ahead, the United Auto Workers (UAW) contract would be up for review; Ford was bracing for the worst. The UAW, as the major alliance of auto workers, had dominated company policies for years, holding management hostage. Historically, the UAW management team ignored the environment of shrinking market share, declining revenues and diminishing profits as they made their demands. Simply put, they had evolved into a powerful political machine.

Anticipating pending negotiations, Ford had leveraged everything it owned to secure a multi-billion dollar credit line as a failsafe against whatever might happen. Impending bankruptcy seemed inevitable. The destruction of Ford Motor Company — an American and global icon — and the rapid deterioration of the American Dream were unfolding right before his eyes. In his role as the company's public relations director, he was trying to convince the world that Ford was in fine shape, but it wasn't. Internal and external communications functioned in crisis management mode. Business was deteriorating rapidly with such a reactive and litigation-avoidance approach.

In early January, Christopher had announced a $12.75 billion annual loss for 2006, the largest loss in the company's storied history. As media critics had pointed out, Ford was losing revenue equivalent to one Mustang every minute!

Christopher, still staring at his computer, was troubled by all of these thoughts, when his phone rang.

"Hey, Chris!" It was Joy, his assistant. "I'm working on the press release for the end of next week, and I need your input. How do we want to spin this?" Christopher paused. The following week marked the 60th anniversary of the passing of Ford Motor Company founder, Henry Ford, who died in his home on April 7, 1947, after a bout with pneumonia. A statement celebrating his life and prominence was required, but as yet unwritten.

"Uh, let me get back to you on that, Joy," Christopher replied. "I'm working through a couple of ideas for that release right now." In recent years, the founder's memorial press releases had been pretty standard. This year, though, Christopher felt that more needed to be done. The heritage of Henry Ford was among the most positive things that the company had going for it. Somehow, he wanted to communicate that message to the public. Henry Ford founded the automobile industry, and in doing so transformed the country from an agricultural era into an industrial one. He enabled the establishment of the middle class in America and was the worker's hero. His story was about innovation, inspiration, teamwork and the American Dream.

This year, times were especially challenging at Ford. Even those closest to the company — including the employees, retirees, dealers, and shareholders — had begun to ask if the company was being true to Henry Ford's vision.

At this crucial moment in the history of Ford, Christopher knew that reminding the public of the company's origins would be more important than ever. Henry Ford had surrounded himself with action-oriented people. He always took a personal interest in his team members and his business. Many referred to Ford Motor Company as Henry Ford's Motor

Company because of his 'get it done' attitude. In contrast, there now appeared to be too much talk but not enough action or sense of urgency.

He stood up from his desk and began pacing back and forth. At the moment, he had no ideas for the press release, and thought that a walk through the Henry Ford Museum might inspire him. With a quick glance out the window, Christopher checked the weather, noting that it was an unusually cold and rainy spring day. Grabbing his coat, he started out the door just as one of the marketing managers came in.

"Hey, how's it going Chris?" asked John. "Got a sec?"

"Sure thing buddy, sit down. So, how's the chemo coming along?" Christopher inquired. John had been fighting a battle against lymphoma for quite some time.

"Well, my cancer markers are going down, but I need more radiation," John answered. "Unfortunately, money's getting tighter all the time. It seems like our health insurance just doesn't cover what it used to. Anyway, there's this new treatment that supposedly has great results for cases as aggressive as mine, but it's real pricey." Christopher's expression turned serious. Then John told him the bad news.

"They let me go today, Chris," said John, lowering his eyes. "Yeah, I'm eligible for early retirement. Guess they'll replace me with some young buck."

Earlier that morning, Christopher had issued a press release about new legislation that would impact retirees, effectively forcing some of them into Medicaid and Medicare with only a small fund to cover deductibles — certainly not the full coverage Ford promised them when they retired. John and many others, it seemed, were being abandoned by the very company they loyally served for so many years. All they had was broken trust and broken dreams.

The news was devastating. Another key person had boarded the brain-drain train of experienced employees being asked to leave Ford through early retirement. Systematically, they were all being replaced by lower salaried people who were young, energetic and promised enormous potential. The problem was that even if you put all the experience of these new hires together, it amounted to no more than a marble rolling down an eight-lane highway — there just wasn't much there. This situation caused more work for longtime employees, who knew plenty and did their jobs rather than inquiring about their next promotion, texting their friends during meetings, or checking Facebook from their office computer. Another hire with long-term potential was great, but when would Ford realize that potential? Ford rarely optimized the potential of new hires. After the company financed their MBAs, these young employees would leave for more attractive offers. In fact, a high percentage of employees with Ford-financed MBA's left the company within five years.

"Don't worry, Chris," John said, noticing the grave expression on Christopher's face. "Everything will work out somehow. It always does. I just wanted you to be one of the first to know."

Christopher paused, then asked, "do you mind if we say a prayer together? I always find that helps, especially during the toughest situations."

John nodded. "That would be great, Chris." Together, they said a quick prayer.

"My wife and I will continue to keep you and your family in our thoughts and prayers," said Christopher. "I'll also keep my eyes and ears open for any job opportunities that might be a good fit. Meanwhile, be sure to let me know if there is anything else I can do."

"You bet," said John. He turned and walked back down the hall.

Now Christopher really needed to clear his head; he certainly wasn't getting any closer to formulating that press release. Grabbing his coat, he headed to the parking garage, taking his company car for a drive to the Henry Ford Museum, a place he visited often. His visits to the museum had always been uplifting and magical; the museum gave credit to ideas born in the minds of the country's greatest, celebrating a God-given gift of human potential that had been realized. It was a true shrine to the real 'doers.' One of his favorite quotes hung atop the large museum door, inscribed on a bronze plaque that read:

*"The highest use of capital is not to make more money, but to
make money to do more for the betterment of life."*
— *Henry Ford*

As he was driving, an unusually dense fog descended, lowering visibility. He could barely see the entrance to the museum's parking lot. Arriving at the gates, he was greeted by a museum guard. Christopher flashed his Ford ID and, once inside, wandered aimlessly through the rooms.

Inside were examples of agricultural equipment, power machinery, and the precursors to the Model T — representing the best of American ingenuity. Each artifact gave a unique insight into the incredible genius of Henry Ford. He walked through exhibits featuring trucks and race cars, heroes of the sky, adventures in early flight, and presidential vehicles — all of which were made in America, unlike most products today.

How could I capture in words the essence of a man who did so much for America and for the world? He thought to himself. *If only I could go back in time and meet this man, who was one of the greatest people in history.* Somehow the message of Henry Ford's legacy, his impact on America, and his vision had to be communicated. This year's statement had to send a strong message of focused efforts, hope, and real action. Christopher lost track of time, until he realized it was nearly noon. Then he decided to head back to the office and grab lunch along the way.

On his way back, he came upon detour signs that twisted and turned him into the rural countryside in the opposite direction of his office. The detours diverted him onto dirt roads winding along farm fields. He did not recall seeing any detour signs before, but assumed they had been placed for the seemingly endless construction that often occurred around Dearborn. Soon everything began to look alike, and he became confused. The peaks of Dearborn's high-rises were fading in the distance. *I must have been heading West,* he thought, noting that the fog was so thick that he could barely see the road in front of him. All he could do was follow the misty glow of his own headlights.

Lost in his thoughts, Christopher recalled his conversation with John, and the involuntary early retirement package presented to his friend at such a critical time of his life. He thought about all the good people, about all the poor decisions by the company, and about his task of spinning the truth and repackaging what was really going on at Ford.

The sky darkened; threatening clouds hovered on the horizon, indicators that a storm was quickly approaching. The car began to lose power, then slowed down to a halt. He grabbed for his cell phone to call his wife Faith, but there was no signal. Buckets of rain pounded the road, and a firing squad of hail shot down. The gusting winds shook his car from side to side. Thunder rumbled and lightning ripped across the fields. He closed his eyes and held onto the little St. Christopher medal hanging from his rearview mirror. An Italian lady had given him the medal when he was a little boy traveling in Rome on a family vacation. She said it would always protect him on his future journeys.

He wasn't sure how long he'd been sitting in his car when the winds died down and the storm finally subsided. Radiant sun broke through the clouds as the colors of a rainbow arched over the road. Christopher turned the key, but the engine wouldn't start. He turned on his car radio, where the only thing that seemed to be working was one AM channel playing scratchy old melodies from days gone by.

Frustrated, and a little concerned, he got out of his car. Alone on the side of the dirt road, he vaguely noticed cows grazing in the meadow and wildflowers along the roadside. He was lost, disoriented; everything seemed so unfamiliar to him.

Christopher started walking down the road to look for help when, suddenly, a car pulled up next to him, seemingly out of nowhere. He did a double take at what looked like a brand new, shiny Model T Ford. Its ebony-lacquered finish and chrome trim gleamed like polished sterling. The man inside waved and leaned over to the passenger side of the car.

"You look to be in quite a pickle there," the man remarked. "What seems to be the problem?"

"Well, my car quit running in the storm, and then my phone stopped working. The only darn thing that works is one AM radio channel, but it's playing some kind of scratchy old-fashioned music from my grandparents' day," replied Christopher.

The man chuckled. "Can I give you a lift? It's no trouble at all. There's a nice place a piece up the road, and you can ring for help from there," he offered.

"Is your cell phone working?" asked Christopher.

The man seemed perplexed at the question and then smiled. "Why don't you just climb on in, young man? I'm sure we can figure this out together."

Christopher looked over at the man in the Model T. For some reason, he looked familiar, though he couldn't recall ever having met him. He was older, a distinguished-looking gentleman, tall and of slight stature — a handsome man with a striking, oval-shaped face of fine-chiseled features. His forehead soared high above kind, inquisitive eyes. Elegantly dressed in fashion of the early 20th century, the man wore an overcoat quite similar to Christopher's and a vintage three-piece suit made from a silk-like fabric. Atop his head of fine graying hair perched a dashing black derby hat. His complexion, though, was somewhat pallid, and he worked at keeping an annoying cough under control.

He noticed that the man's radio was also tuned into an AM station, playing the same old-fashioned songs as the one he'd heard on his own car radio. Admiring the pristine condition of the antique car, Christopher asked in childish awe, "wow, what a car! Are you an antique car collector?"

"I guess you could say that," replied the man. "I've got plenty more where this came from. Mass production is a wonderful phenomenon!"

"Man, the guys back at the general office would sure like to see one of these in person. We don't make them like this anymore," exclaimed Christopher.

"You're in the automobile business too?" the stranger inquired.

"Yes. I've been with Ford for a quarter of a century. You might say it's been my life."

The man raised an eyebrow and winked.

"You and I just might have quite a lot to talk about. I've delved into the car business myself. I used to work at Ford years ago. You could say it was my life too. How about you and I have some lunch together while we're waiting on someone to help with your car?" the man suggested. "We're almost there."

Christopher looked out at the countryside rolling by, not realizing just how far they had driven. Ahead was the famous Fairlane Manor, once the home of Henry Ford. Renovated many years ago, the manor was now a popular restaurant and conference center. As the man drove to the front of the Estate, an attendant hustled out to greet them and open the man's door. After they both had climbed out, the attendant parked the car. Together they walked through the iron gates of Fairlane Manor and into the grand entrance hall. The rooms were oddly empty. Though he had visited the manor on many occasions, things looked very different this time.

Maybe they're redecorating or filming a movie or something, he thought.

A tuxedoed waiter quickly appeared, offering to take their coats and the man's derby, which he neatly placed in the cloakroom.

"Will you be dining in the private hall today, sir?" inquired the waiter.

"Yes, that will be fine. Thank you, Albert," the man answered. "And I'd sure appreciate it if you'd see to taking care of my friend's car which got stranded up along Greenfield Village Road, near Molly's farm, after the storm."

Nodding, the attendant left the room. The two men walked down an extensive hallway and into the dining room, where old masters' paintings and statues adorned the corner nooks and walls. They were seated at a formally appointed table beside a huge stone fireplace. A roaring fire spread a blanket of nostalgic warmth into the dampness of the room. Christopher glanced down at his watch. Although he knew it must be past noon by now, his watch read seven o'clock on the dot. At that moment, the towering grandfather clock in the entry hall began to chime, echoing throughout the manor. On the seventh chime, the clock stopped. A melancholy quiet enveloped Fairlane Manor. He thought that perhaps the tired old clock and even his own wristwatch had somehow been affected by the strange storm.

"Never confuse activity with accomplishment." — *Mr. Carman*

CHAPTER THIRTEEN

THE ROAD TO BANKRUPTCY?

"Failure is simply the opportunity to begin again,
this time more intelligently."
— Henry Ford

"WILL IT BE the usual today, Mr. Carman?" the waiter asked. "You bet," the man replied.

"Christopher, I recommend you try some of the fresh vegetables from the greenhouse. More than 36 varieties are grown here at Fairlane Manor." At that, the waiter pulled a cart of what seemed like dozens of fresh and cooked vegetables to the side of the table.

"You know what Will Rogers used to say?" the man chuckled. "He used to say that 'an onion can make people cry, but there has never been a vegetable invented to make them laugh!'"

"Will Rogers?" laughed Christopher. "I have a book of all his quotes. Why, he was one of the wittiest humorists of his time!"

The man nodded and smiled.

"I also recommend the tomato juice with soybean sauce to start," he suggested. "The country-style chicken pie made with homegrown soybeans flavored with garlic and dill is one of my favorites. Soybeans are the healthiest food you can eat, young man! You could also try the fresh-out-of-the-oven soybean cookies and soybean sorbet for dessert."

"That all sounds great," said Christopher. "I'll have that."

The waiter nodded, then walked away to prepare their orders.

"Henry Ford was right-on about the value of soybeans. He was a visionary — a man ahead of his times. Why, I was just reading an article the other day about the profound benefits of soy on human health, like heart health, healthy bones, preventing cancer, lowering cholesterol and other benefits," remarked Christopher.

The man raised an eyebrow and winked. "Henry Ford sure knew what he was talking about, didn't he!" he exclaimed with a smile.

"He certainly did," Christopher agreed.

"So, now that I know your name, Mr. Carman, I guess you should know mine," said Christopher, glad that the waiter had let him know his rescuer's name. "I'm Christopher Hope."

He reached out his hand to Mr. Carman.

"Pleasure to meet you, Christopher," Mr. Carman replied, shaking his hand. "Actually, I have collected several nicknames over the years. People also like to call me Mr. Farmer and Mr. Inventor. But, since we are both in the automobile business, why don't you just call me Mr. Carman?"

"Great to meet you then as well, Mr. Carman," he exclaimed. "So, do you lunch here often?" Christopher inquired, intrigued and impressed with the formality of the setting and the kind hospitality.

"As a matter of fact, I do. This is one of my favorite places. It's home to me," replied Mr. Carman.

"Please, tell me more about yourself," Christopher prodded.

"Besides being an antique car collector, what other interests do you pursue? You seem to be a worldly man. There's something about being here with you at Fairlane Manor. The chance of you coming to my rescue on the road is extraordinary. Maybe it's my destiny to meet you today. I'm very fortunate and grateful to you, Mr. Carman," he said, while searching his mind for a rational explanation. Mr. Carman smiled warmly.

"There's no such thing as chance, Christopher," he replied. "I believe God is managing fate and that he doesn't need any advice from us. With God in charge, I believe everything will work out for the best in the end. So, what is there to worry about? I don't see myself as a worldly man, but thanks for the compliment. I consider myself a simple man. I appreciate nature and its miracles, and I value hard work. But most importantly, I am a patriotic American who believes in the Puritan work ethic and the Jeffersonian principles on which this great nation was founded. I believe that opportunity will not overlook a man because he is wearing overalls. I have a passion for engineering and for the automobile. My interests keep me busy. Gardening. Car collecting. Thinking up new inventions. Traveling. I grew up on a farm not far from here and I have never left my roots."

Christopher felt at home with his new acquaintance. He was eager to share his thoughts and concerns with him, and somehow felt that speaking with him could make a real difference. He wasn't sure why, but somehow this man might hold the keys to doors he had been hoping to open.

"As a Ford man, you may be able to bring me up to speed about the company today, the automobile industry, and the customers' perceptions of both," said Mr. Carman. "I have a personal interest, a stake you could say, in knowing the real story about the current state of the Ford Motor Company."

"I'm just a small fish in a big pond, but I would appreciate sharing my points of view with you," Christopher answered. "I'm the vice-president of public relations at Ford. For many years now, I've had my hand on the pulse of the company's internal and external communications, processing news, communicating and managing it — and unfortunately *spinning* it as needed for today's circumstances. As I see it, Ford is suffering from a series of problems — unfair trade practices, lack of leadership, compensation that is not tied to productivity, bad alliances and deals, over-engineering, diversity gone astray, and many more issues. Recovery will take several years for sure.

"This past January, we reported an annual loss in 2006 of $12.75 billion — that's billion with a capital B. That's $400 per second, $24,100 per minute, $1,450,000 per hour, and $34,795,000 per day! Ford would have done just as well to give every person on planet earth two dollars each last year. Some analysts even estimate that given the table limits, it would have been cheaper for the company to send all of our North American employees to Las Vegas and let them gamble twenty-four hours a day, 365 days of the year. The company would have most likely come out in a better financial position. The amount of money the company lost in dollar bills would stretch 1.23 million miles. Stacked end to end, 12.75 billion dollar bills could wrap around the world 49 times or make two and a half trips to the moon! The amount of loss is incredible!"

Mr. Carman raised his eyebrows. "Las Vegas? Two and a half trips to the moon? Four hundred dollars a second?" he said, aghast, shaking his head feverishly back and forth. "Why, $400 is about what one Ford automobile cost when they were first produced!" Mr. Carman continued listening intently and seemed to hang on every word.

"The U.S. automotive industry today is drastically over-regulated," Christopher continued. "Foreign competitors enjoy much lower labor costs, government-subsidized healthcare benefits, unfair trade practices and the U.S. free market 'fend-for-yourself' syndrome. Other countries tightly restrict our trade. To make things more challenging, the media glorifies Toyota and Honda, making them media darlings. Heck, even the Motor City press favors the foreign transplants."

"Is that so?" asked Mr. Carman. "Why, in my day, things that were happening at Ford were the biggest news around! I wonder why that's changed."

"The media has created a false perception that our foreign rivals have a product quality advantage," explained Christopher. "In reality, though, the facts show otherwise. The media could help change that perception by telling the truth about Toyota's engine sludge concerns in tens of thousands of Toyota products. Many Toyota engines of the model years 1997 to 2002 produced major sludge that caused premature engine failure, costing consumers big time. Toyota did not stand behind the products that had this problem, leaving tens of thousands of customers with cars needing expensive repair. Still, they received a pass from the media. In fact, it even seems the media partnered with them to help them get away with defrauding the American public. Toyota finally agreed to settle the case, but denies there was ever a problem. As a matter of fact, Toyota recalled more vehicles than they sold during 2006, but that was hardly even mentioned in the U.S. media.

"In addition, it was reported that over 800,000 Toyota Tacoma's and Tundra's did not have adequate corrosion protection, causing the frames to literally disintegrate from rust. Once again, customers are left holding the bag for expensive repairs and devalued trades. Do you think the media even paid attention to this, even though they've known about it for several years? No! The media playing favorites with foreign auto manufacturers has hurt American manufacturers, resulting in the loss of many American jobs. This is not just critical to Ford, this is about an entire industry that is vitally important to America. This is about ensuring that our country has a strong manufacturing base and about ensuring national security. This is something everyone in our country has a vested interest in."

"Loss of American jobs?" said Mr. Carman. "Yes, I am aware of this crisis. I can certainly understand your point that the media's favoritism to foreign manufacturers is contributing to this problem. Is Ford doing anything to change this?"

"Well, actually, American auto companies need to do a much better job of changing the public's perception on their own because we cannot rely on the U.S. media for any favors," said Christopher. "Unfortunately, though, we don't tell the Ford story very well, and when we do, the media doesn't seem to pay much attention to it. I don't understand why even the Motor City press would seem to take such joy in bashing the American auto companies upon which so many people in their home market depend for their livelihood."

"In my day, foreign manufacturers looked to American companies as examples — as leaders," said Mr. Carman.

"That's true," Christopher replied. "Ironically, Ford and Toyota have a long association that stretches back over five decades. In fact, Ford allowed managers from Toyota, which was trying to regroup after World War II, to study the operations at its giant Rouge complex in Dearborn. These visits actually helped them develop the famed Toyota production system, which emphasizes driving out waste, fostering worker involvement, and making continuous improvements on the factory floor. The very systems that Toyota is renowned for were modeled after good old American systems from Ford — but the public doesn't even know it. So, they give all the credit to the Japanese.

"Toyota also came to Ford first in the 1980's, when it was looking for an American partner with which to open its first U.S. plant. The two companies held brief discussions that could have led to a joint venture to build a midsize car for each company. At the time, Ford didn't believe that the partnership would provide much benefit to them, considering the high cost of the venture. So instead, Toyota entered into a joint venture with GM which to this day is Toyota's only unionized automotive assembly plant.

"Toyota was originally the world's leader in hybrid electric cars and previously licensed hybrid technology to Ford, which we used in a small

SUV. However, Ford now has its own hybrid electric and flex-fuel technology and is considered an industry leader in these areas."

"There is no reason for Ford to be tied to any other automobile manufacturer," insisted Mr. Carman. "Our people have always been some of the best and brightest in the world."

"Our current President and CEO, Alan Mulally, is very knowledgeable about this area," Christopher continued. "He happens to be a student of the Toyota production system and used a form of it on assembly lines at Boeing, which he ran before joining Ford last year. I believe there is something that differentiates Mulally from his predecessors at Ford — something very refreshing and extremely optimistic. He comes across as a common man who is truly interested in the automobile industry and in people, much like Henry Ford was. Mulally is an exceptionally positive person, a true servant leader in every sense. In challenging times like these, people need to see hope, and he articulates hope better than anyone. His optimism is so infectious that you sometimes have to remind yourself of the huge challenges ahead. But rest assured, sir, behind his relentlessly upbeat appearance is a very intense and focused businessman. He is absolutely the right leader at the right time for Ford. I think he is the real deal — call it destiny that he came in at a time such as this," finished Christopher.

"He sounds like the man with the plan," Mr. Carman said. "Please continue, young man."

"Why just this morning I received an internal memo further illustrating the uneven playing field between Ford and foreign manufacturers," Christopher explained. "The memo details a recent audit of Ford's books which revealed that at least one-third of the cities that Ford has facilities in overcharged us on 2006 city taxes to the tune of millions of dollars. When Ford asked about recovering these overcharges, most cities indicated that they didn't have the money to reimburse Ford. Furthermore, in many cases, Ford was told that if the cities in question did reimburse them, they would have to raise property taxes to make up for the lost revenue from Ford. Such decisions would require a voters' referendum, taking as long as two years. Meanwhile, some of the same cities that were overcharging Ford were offering foreign transplant companies up to fifteen years of special tax breaks as incentives to bring manufacturing jobs to their area. To cover these tax-free years — you guessed it — property taxes were raised. So, in short, the property taxes paid in some cities are actually subsidizing foreign automobile companies while at the same time overcharging American companies like Ford and resulting in the loss of more American jobs."

"You know, son," said Mr. Carman. "When the automobile industry was created, it opened the door to many competitors. Uneven playing fields aside, in such a highly competitive industry, you have to consistently play at a higher level to win the game. Many companies are not around today because they lost focus and vision and were not held accountable for decisions. Whether you are the leader of a corporation or the leader of a nation, loss is not only measured in terms of dollars, it is measured by human stagnation and the inability to improve the lives of people. It's simple math. A business that makes nothing but money is a poor kind of business. It's not the employer who pays wages — he only handles the money. It is the product that pays the wages. If you are bankrupt in ideas, vision, and product, you will soon be bankrupt financially, and your employees, partners, and customers will pay the price. When leaders care more about money than doing the right things and providing a great place to work, then the business is doomed to fail."

"I wonder what Henry Ford would think if he were sitting here with us today," said Christopher in a reflective tone. Mr. Carman leaned back in his chair and nodded. He had a rather misty look in his eyes.

Christopher sensed that Mr. Carman must be an admirer of Henry Ford. He dressed and even looked like him. The resemblance was quite remarkable, but Christopher brushed off the notion as simply a twinge of nostalgia. In any case, whomever this stranger was, he had hit the nail right on the head. Somehow, Mr. Carman understood what was happening at Ford. Christopher took out a small notepad and pen, suddenly thinking that taking notes would be a good idea. The new-found wisdom from this charismatic man should be recorded.

"Mr. Carman, do you mind if I take notes from our conversation?" he asked. "Next week is the 60th anniversary of the passing of Henry Ford — April 7th to be exact. Every year we issue a press release, and I want to make this year's release particularly significant. I want to write about Henry Ford's vision. That's what the American public needs to be reminded of, now more than ever. You seem to think so much the way he did, that I thought perhaps you would be able to inspire me in recreating his message."

At that moment, the room grew colder, and the lights dimmed. Mr. Carman took a neatly starched, cotton handkerchief out of his vest pocket. Christopher noticed two initials embroidered on it but couldn't make them out. Mr. Carman excused himself, put the handkerchief to his mouth, and began to cough. His face grew pale. The fire slowed its furious pace, burning down to crumbling embers. Suddenly chilled to his bones, Christopher could see a vale of vapor from his own breath.

"Getting cold in here… there must be a problem with the heating or electricity," Christopher remarked. Mr. Carman didn't seem to hear him. The waiter quickly entered the dining room carrying a cup of steaming liquid.

"Here, sir, drink this. It will help settle down your cough." Mr. Carman sipped the hot brew slowly; his cough began to subside.

"Great stuff this is, soybean tea. They grow these soybeans right here on this estate. You should try some. It'll cure what ails you," said Mr. Carman.

"I'd love a cup," replied Christopher, and Albert left to get him one. As he drank the tea, he suddenly felt warmer and stronger. He could understand why Mr. Carman was so fond of his soybean tea.

"Mr. Carman, I have a great opportunity to tell the real story of what's going on at the company," he continued, suddenly feeling the need to confide in this mysterious stranger. "In addition to the press release, I am working with a reporter at a Detroit paper on a series of stories about issues concerning the future of Ford. I feel compelled to tell the truth, no matter what it might cost me personally. You have years of experience, as a former company man who was with the company when Henry Ford's leadership and vision were more consistent with company truths. Maybe you could help me sort out my thoughts and give me feedback and insights from your perspective of Henry Ford's original vision."

Mr. Carman smiled. "This means a lot to me," he said. "I'd be happy to assist in any way I can. When I was at the company, we had a clear vision that was true to the company's humble beginnings. From what you have just told me, I can see that some of that original vision has been lost. But there isn't much time. I have only a few days left before I must travel on. Still, I have a vested interest in the company for many reasons on a personal level, reasons that I might tell you more about later. I may even invite some friends of mine to join us who may add value to your search for the truth. Why don't we make lunch here a standing appointment each day for the next week or so?"

Christopher quickly agreed to the lunch meetings. Even though he knew he would have to clear his calendar, he did not want to miss any opportunity to share in Mr. Carman's wisdom. He had an uncanny notion that he was on the right road to finding what he was looking for. Reenergized like a crusader on a noble quest, he found his spirits lifted.

"Albert will take you to your car. I am sure you'll find it's in fine condition now," said Mr. Carman with a slight knowing smile.

Christopher's mouth gaped open. He had almost completely forgotten about his car and the mysterious circumstances that had brought him to Fairlane Manor that day. "Well, that was quick," he recovered. "I expected to wait a couple of hours for roadside assistance to get here. Much appreciated. Is there any way I can repay you?"

Mr. Carman smiled, "Not today. This one is on the house."

Albert helped Christopher on with his coat.

Again, Mr. Carman began to cough.

It was time to go.

"I'll see you tomorrow, same time, same place," Mr. Carman told Christopher.

"Some say adversity builds character.
I believe adversity reveals one's character."
— *Mr. Carman*

CHAPTER TWELVE

LEADERSHIP

"Coming together is a beginning; keeping together is progress;
working together is success."
— *Henry Ford*

A SUDDEN STORM FORESHADOWED a series of unusual circumstances that led to a random meeting with a mysterious stranger on a dirt road. The sun was shining brightly, and the sky was Ford blue as far as the eye could see. The detour road signs were gone, and Christopher found himself driving right back on the main road towards Dearborn.

He reached for his phone, which was working now, and dialed his wife's cell number.

"Hey honey, it's me. Yeah, I know. Sorry I didn't call you earlier. No Faith, I didn't shut my phone off. That bad storm must have knocked down the cell towers. Any damage to the house from the storm? The winds were so strong that my car was pushed to the side of the road. I'm not sure what happened after that and then a man drove by out of nowhere and…"

But before he could finish telling her everything that had happened that morning, Faith interrupted him.

"Honey, please slow down. What storm are you talking about? The weather in Dearborn has been beautiful all morning — sunny and clear skies. I watched the Weather Channel this morning, and as a matter of fact the forecast called for clear weather across the whole state today and right through the next week! Where are you? Sure you're okay?"

Christopher paused for a moment.

"Yeah, don't worry, I'm doing fine… I've had an incredible day. I'll tell you all about it later tonight."

He turned on his car radio to his usual FM station; everything seemed to be back to normal, or was it really? Perhaps the weather was calm now, but Christopher felt the winds of change blowing through Dearborn. Somehow he knew that, after today, things would never be quite the same.

Back at his office that afternoon, he found a copy of an archived news article on his desk. With it was a note from Frank McIntyre. He cringed, suddenly remembering that he had promised to be available for Frank's call earlier that morning. Frank must have dropped by in person, as he often did when he was working on an important piece. The article which Frank had left on his desk had appeared in the Detroit paper more than a year ago. It talked about Ford slashing 28 percent of its workforce in a sweeping bid to save itself.

Christopher recalled the article well — it had caused quite a stir in the higher levels of Ford's leadership. Frank's note read: "Christopher, we need to address the issue of Ford's declining workforce. How is Ford planning to come out of this one?"

He sank into his chair and re-read the article. It painted a bleak future for the company, a future that was slowly being realized. It said that Ford was staking its future on the success of a gut-wrenching restructuring of its North American operations, a move that would dramatically downsize the number two U.S. automaker. It also said that the company was mired in one of the deepest crises in its 102-year history.

Ford had unveiled its long-awaited Way Forward plan to slash up to 30,000 manufacturing jobs, cut 4,000 salaried employees, and shutter 14 factories. Bill Ford, Chairman and CEO at the time, was quoted saying that these cuts were a painful last resort, and he was deeply mindful of their impact, affecting many lives, many families, and many communities. There was a graph with the article showing investor reaction and stock prices falling by half from 2002 to year-end 2005. The predictions seemed to be coming true, a self-fulfilling prophecy.

So much more had happened in one year — more layoffs, more cuts, more debt, and more bad news. Christopher went on-line, pulling up the company's three-year stock price history from January 2004 to January 2007. His screen flashed up a similarly bleak chart.

Sitting at his desk, he held his head in his hands for a moment. Then he printed out the stock chart and put the press article and stock chart in his pocket so he would remember to show them to Mr. Carman. Only a few hours remained before the end of the workday. Christopher decided to type up a few of his notes from his earlier meeting with Mr. Carman.

With a gleam in his eye, he picked up the phone and called his assistant, Joy.

"Hey Joy, it's me. About the press release… I think I have a handle on this year's spin. Let's title it something to the effect of *This Year Marks the 60th Anniversary of Henry Ford's Passing — A Year Unlike Any Other in Ford Motor Company's History*. Let's communicate the genius of our founder and the company's commitment to turn things around. Let's throw them a curve ball — positive, positive, positive!"

He jotted down a few ideas for the annual press release. After an unusually quiet late afternoon, he closed up his office and headed home.

The next day, Christopher arrived right on time for his appointment with Mr. Carman. As he pulled up to the gates of Fairlane Manor, the temperature dropped and the winds suddenly picked up. Mr. Carman was waiting for him, sitting in a rocking chair, reading a newspaper on the front porch. The attendant met Christopher at his car as Mr. Carman put down his newspaper and waved. Approaching the porch, he thought he heard Mr. Carman mumble something to himself like "incredible, just incredible!"

"What would that be, Mr. Carman?" he asked.

"Christopher, the possibilities in today's world are endless," remarked Mr. Carman. "You know, in all my life, I could not discover anyone who knew enough to say what is and what is not possible!"

Upon entering the manor, they handed Albert their coats. As they walked past the old grandfather clock in the entrance, it chimed seven single tones just as it had the day before. Mr. Carman glanced up at the clock and Christopher glanced down at his watch. The hour hand on his watch was once again stuck at seven. He had only recently replaced the battery and the jeweler said his watch was in perfect working order.

The appetizing aromas coming from the dining room and the cozy smell of wood burning in the fireplace soon made him forget about the time. The dining table was formally set, as it had been the day before. It seemed as though not a single moment had passed since his first meeting with Mr. Carman the previous day. Albert arrived at their table to take their orders.

"I'll have the usual, Albert," requested Mr. Carman in his polite and unassuming manner," and soybean tea of course — it'll help this nagging cough. Just can't seem to get it under control today."

"And you, sir?" asked Albert.

"The same as Mr. Carman," he replied.

"I like a man who knows what he wants," Mr. Carman smiled warmly.

Christopher removed his notepad and pen from his jacket pocket and placed them on the table in front of him.

"I'd really like to hear more about the leadership team at Ford," said Mr. Carman. "Have they produced any leaders that my generation would be proud of — people of integrity and common sense, who place the well-being of the common man as the main focus in their leadership decisions?"

"I brought something to show you, Mr. Carman," he said, pulling out a newspaper article and a stock chart. He placed the copies on the table, and pointed to the title of the article. "Ford leadership, you ask?" said Christopher. "This article writes about Ford's series of very poor decisions that are finally taking their toll. I found this article on my desk yesterday morning. Frank, the reporter I was telling you about, left it for me. It seems he wants to address these layoffs in the piece he is working on."

Mr. Carman furrowed his brow as he read through the article, glanced at the graphs, then he handed them back, sensing that Christopher was upset by the bleak picture the article and graphs painted for Ford. "Seems like they're turning the American dream into a nightmare."

Christopher just shook his head.

"I'm listening," encouraged Mr. Carman. "Tell me more about Ford's leadership in recent years."

Christopher took in a deep breath and sighed. "At Ford, there have been many years of very little accountability. Senior managers have been highly compensated but their pay is not linked to results. The same is true for UAW workers. Their compensation is often not tied to results either. Overly dominant senior managers with disdain for both employee and customer input have been steering the company. Management teams seem more interested in being politically correct than in getting profitable results. There are no perceived rewards for the business generators, the rainmakers. This system has produced managers who move along without accomplishing much of anything. In turn, many of our Ford managers confuse activity with accomplishments and spend half their time telling you what they are going to do and the other half explaining why they didn't get it done. Since their compensation is not tied directly to performance, the necessary accountability is not there."

He paused to see Mr. Carman's reaction to what he had said. Mr. Carman was markedly distraught, fueling Christopher's passion even more.

"Furthermore, the arrogance of some of our former senior managers left us with limited effectiveness in dealing with our retail partners — the dealers. Our managers seemed isolated from the real world at times, and didn't appear to value what really happened at the retail level. Also, asking for help or feedback within Ford has been deemed a sign of weakness. It's the 'emperor-has-no-clothes' syndrome where many managers ignore employee involvement and participative management because it's too time consuming and requires that managers leave their kingdom…but it wasn't always this way."

"Tell me more about the sales force," Mr. Carman requested. "Are they knowledgeable, and are they given the support they need from company management to acquire the skills to do the best job they can and make sure that the customer gets the best product out there for a fair price? Have they been empowered to make the right decisions?"

"It's been a long time since Ford has provided any meaningful hands-on sales training to the company or dealership employees," Christopher replied. "Many of the seasoned employees remember when our selling ability was what led us to market share gains and sales leadership. Today's managers, who lack sales training, seem to fall back on a crystal ball mentality. They constantly look to future products that they hope will make up for their inability to sell the current ones. There's a recurring theme: 'Wait until the new products come out within the next eighteen months. The new products are going to be dynamite. Ford leaders play this wait-and-see game over and over again, just like an old record stuck in a groove.

"There is a sales skills deficiency in the company and very little acknowledgment or recognition of it," Christopher continued. "The marketing mantra evolved into a single idea of selling 'the deal' versus selling the car. This type of thinking is a costly and risky proposition because it demands putting big time incentive money on the hoods, and has you gambling on the next product being a superstar.

"Another problem is that top management in recent years lacked vision and the ability to lead. They handed too much of the reins of the company over to the finance people. It seemed that their strategy was simply to cut costs at every corner and to transfer as many costs as possible to our dealers and suppliers. The backbone of our business — our valuable partnerships with our dealers and suppliers — was put at risk.

"Lack of proper empowerment and a litigation-avoidance strategy were far too often creating paralysis-by-analysis for our pencil pushers in Detroit, who were responsible for creating flashy reports rather than profits."

He sensed Mr. Carman was quite concerned and could tell that his questions were far more poignant than they had been the day before. Mr. Carman's cough began to worsen.

"It sounds like management at Ford is doing the opposite of what I would have advised," replied Mr. Carman. "They are operating under an unrealistic assessment of their own abilities. They are robbing the future today. Many people think that by hoarding the decision-making power and money, they are gaining safety for themselves. In fact, if money is your only hope for independence, you will never have it. The only real security that a person can have in this world is a reserve of knowledge, experience, and ability. Without these qualities, money is practically useless. Remember, Christopher, very few people are born great. They achieve greatness through inspiration, vision and good old-fashioned hard work."

Christopher nodded in agreement.

"I'll give you an example of robbing the future," said Christopher. "A former CEO basically robbed our product development," Christopher ventured. "He came from Europe and believed that we were overcompensated in North America. He felt that we paid too much attention to the North American market. He forced the shift of resources away from the U.S. market, which made up the vast majority of our business! He focused our resources on the international market, which at the time accounted for very little of our vehicle sales and even less of our earnings. Then, following his leadership was another guy, also from Europe. He said he wanted the company to become more of a consumer products company. In a classic case of Ford not handling success very well, we took our eye off the ball. It seemed when we were profitable, and things were really rolling in our favor, we had a tendency to lose focus on keeping the main thing, the main thing. Under this GE Jack Welch clone, we squandered billions on ill-conceived diversification schemes that were later sold off for pennies on the dollar. He tried to make Ford more of a marketing company instead of a manufacturing company. After wasting billions of dollars, he was paid millions to leave.

"These top leaders made decisions without regard to the fact that their negative impact would linger for years. Leaders failed to follow through on important new product plans causing us to lose significant market share. Furthermore, Ford sometimes used fuzzy math internally to determine year-to-year profitability, ignoring capital investment cost."

"Did top executives get paid huge bonuses using this new math you talk about, ignoring the cost of capital investment?" Mr. Carman asked.

"Yes, sir, I believe they did!" Christopher exclaimed. "This is like our elected officials in the United States Congress and Senate making all the decisions on current and future programs such as Social Security and proposed national health care while knowing full well that these programs won't affect them one bit. They're under a much more lucrative system."

"Sounds like 'do as I say, not as I do,'" quipped Mr. Carman.

"While double standards exist today," continued Christopher. "The American automobile companies can no longer afford to operate like a governmental entity. At some point, the shareholders will ask how Ford stock can be in the tank in only a few years while the company is paying out big salaries and bonuses to top executives who have achieved very little improvement in tangible objective results. At the same time, we are pushing some of our talented mid-level managers out to early retirement, then hiring lower salary entry-level employees with very little experience. We should be keeping our top performers and paying them well, instead of hiring low-level, inexperienced employees and overpaying senior managers who are not performing."

"It appears that the monkeys are running the zoo," Mr. Carman jested.

Christopher laughed. "Sometimes it feels that way."

"Why you know what a famous writer used to say," said Mr. Carman with a grin, "If there were nothing wrong in the world, there wouldn't be anything for us to do." Christopher grimaced. "Mr. Carman, our leaders quit listening to our loyal dealers and customers, the people behind our success. They started to believe that success was based on them as leaders and they discounted the importance of the dealers who drive our business. Now, listen to another example of a very costly experiment. With the advent of the world wide web and our ownership of several dot-com operations, some of our senior leaders thought we could 'go it alone' without the dealers. Armed with the arrogance of a wholesale experience, and the naïveté and over-confidence that comes from a lack of understanding of the value of retail operational expertise and local relationships, they set out to create the Ford Retail Network (FRN). They went into Salt Lake City and Tulsa, and bought out established dealers. They replaced the dealership management teams with Ford managers equipped primarily with untested theories and little retail experience. This project disrupted well-established Ford dealers and replaced them with ones that sold about half of the Ford vehicles as the prior ones. Eventually, we sold these stores back to retail dealer organizations for a fraction of what we paid for them."

Mr. Carman shook his head in disbelief. He leaned across the table. "Christopher, don't they know we'd be nothing without our great dealer partners? It's they who employ and provide for their communities. It's they who support their local organizations and charities. Ford and Lincoln Mercury dealers are the face of Ford in communities across America."

Christopher could tell he'd struck a delicate nerve with Mr. Carman. Lowering his voice, Christopher proceeded. "In the 1980's, we had leaders that made decisive calls to refresh our products. They were bright, bold leaders. In my opinion, it was when they retired that the problems began. There was no good succession plan in place to continue their leadership. At the time, the most qualified leader we had was passed over for personal reasons. So the company pulled in their second choice to do the job. He was a rough guy with little charisma, but he was willing to do the job. He was up against Lee Iacocca at Chrysler, who had actually been hired by Henry Ford II, but was released because he was seen as a threat to the Ford family. Iacocca was a brilliant leader, though he admittedly had quite an ego. That left us with a second stringer against a superstar."

"Lack of succession planning has been a downfall for many companies," exclaimed Mr. Carman, struggling to keep his composure. "It's important that there always be a successor in place to perpetuate the values and vision of the company."

"You are right, sir. Bet there won't be a succession plan issue on Mulally's watch," Christopher continued, "In addition, we exacerbate the problem because we seem to say goodbye to our retirees rather than keep them in the loop on important happenings at the company. They are a very large group of loyal and productive citizens, scattered across America, contributing in their communities. Most of them bleed 'Ford blue.' They belong to retiree groups like Fair Alliance and F.R.E.E., and we ought to reach out and listen to them more often. After all, many of them spent their entire working lives at Ford and still have lots of great ideas and passion for our company.

"Shortly after the 9/11 terrorist attack on the United States, Henry Ford's great-grandson, Bill Ford, Jr., became the CEO. Life had changed suddenly, not only at Ford, but everywhere in our great country after that horrific terrorist attack. Bill Ford was asked by the Ford family to step forward and indeed he did. He could easily have opted out of taking on such a difficult challenge but the family business and America needed him in these unprecedented times. It was Ford leading the way along side GM and Chrysler after that fateful day — 9/11/01. The Detroit Three came together with a ZERO percent financing offer to do their part in keeping commerce going. It was a great example of how important the American automobile industry is to our nation's economy," Christopher paused. "Did you know that analysts estimate that at least one out of every seven people in America are directly or indirectly employed by the automobile industry today?" he asked.

Mr. Carman smiled. "Hmm, very impressive. That special financing offer was quite a noble effort! Sure makes you proud to be an American."

"Absolutely," Christopher agreed. "After a successful stint at the top, Bill Ford knew it was time to hand over the reins. His executive search landed at the doorstep of Boeing's Alan Mulally. Mulally is credited with the turn-around of the Commercial Airplanes division of the Boeing company. His legacy is based on achieving 83 percent of the market share in the airplane industry. Analysts say that he had a terrific record in managing a manufacturing assembly type business and that he had an exemplary performance record under very difficult circumstances. However, in the airplane industry, there are only two real competitors in commercial airlines — Boeing and Airbus. On the other hand, the automotive industry is fiercely regulated by the government and foreign subsidized labor outside the U.S. It's a tricky environment we're in and nothing like the aircraft industry. Hopefully, Mulally can transfer his leadership skills to Ford and help pull us out of the spot we're in. He's the best chance we have right now."

He thought he heard Mr. Carman utter something under his breath.

"I told them, I told them."

"You told who what?" he asked, trying to understand Mr. Carman's last sentence.

"Those who should have listened," replied Mr. Carman, who was clearly struggling to hold down his frustration as his cough worsened. His breathing became shallow and he tried not to cough.

Christopher hadn't realized how emotionally involved Mr. Carman was in what he had to say. He knew there must be a deeper connection to Ford than Mr. Carman had initially let on.

Albert appeared almost out of nowhere to tend to Mr. Carman, bringing with him another dose of the steaming tea.

It was time to go. Christopher stood up to excuse himself and walked toward the cloakroom to fetch his coat.

"I'll see you tomorrow then, Christopher, same time, same place," Mr. Carman said in a rasped voice.

"Servant leaders don't think less of themselves, they just think of themselves less." — Mr. Carman

CHAPTER ELEVEN

BRAND MANAGEMENT

"The man who will use his skill and constructive imagination
to see how much he can give for a dollar,
instead of how little he can give for a dollar,
is bound to succeed." — Henry Ford

WHEN CHRISTOPHER ARRIVED at Fairlane Manor for his next lunch meeting with the intriguing and mysterious Mr. Carman, he noticed a magnificently pristine Model T antique car parked right in front of the manor. It was a different model from the one Mr. Carman had rescued him in the other day. The engine was running, and the hood of the impeccable black beauty was propped open. Mr. Carman was bent down beside the car, admiring it.

"Come on over here, young man," Mr. Carman motioned to him when he saw him approaching. "Take a look at a real work of art. Do you know how many American workers were involved in making this engine? It's like a finely-tuned symphony orchestra, and when it all comes together, what beautiful music it makes! Just listen to it purr. Everyone who drove one of these cars back in my day knew that it was very reliable and if anything went wrong, it would be fixed quickly and to their satisfaction.

"You must believe in your products and stand behind them, putting your customers first," Mr. Carman explained as he gently closed the hood.

"Every time I take a look at this engine, I think of the millions of Americans whose quality of life has been improved by this vehicle. You see, the primary purpose of industry and ingenuity is to serve the common man and improve living standards for every single person on this earth. If ideas and inventions such as the automobile are born from a scheme to get rich, then we have failed others and ultimately ourselves," said Mr. Carman.

At that moment, Christopher noticed that Mr. Carman was wearing a heavier jacket than usual today. His complexion seemed more pale and his breathing shallower than the day before.

"Are you okay?" inquired Christopher, worried about the worsening condition of Mr. Carman's cough.

"Thank you, but I think some warm lunch and a nice hot cup of soybean tea will fix it!" Mr. Carman replied.

Albert was waiting for them inside the entrance and offered to take their coats. The men walked side by side into the dining hall, where the splendid fire cast its warm glow throughout the large room.

"I'll have the usual, Albert," said Mr. Carman. Christopher nodded to Albert, signifying he'd again be having the same as his new friend. He was becoming quite fond of the delicious meals and tea they shared at the manor, each featuring soybeans as a star ingredient.

Christopher placed his pen and notepad on the table, not wanting to waste any time, especially since Mr. Carman had mentioned that he was leaving on a journey in only a few days.

"Son, have you ever heard of a snake oil salesman?" Mr. Carman began. "Back in my day, we had such a thing. These characters looked sharp and talked fast. They tried real hard to make you think that somehow they knew better than you. They spent a great deal of time and effort trying to convince you their products were the best and to get you to buy them. In reality, all they really wanted was to take your money."

"I think I know what you mean, Mr. Carman," Christopher replied.

"In fact," Christopher continued. "Modern-day snake oil salesmen are sometimes called consultants. They charge millions but provide little if any helpful advice, strategy, or solutions. And, by the way, their pay is usually not tied to results in any way. Brand management consultants, for example, tricked Ford leaders into making many poor decisions that have cost Ford greatly. Ford executives sometimes seem bewitched by the myth of brand management, the 21st century version of snake oil.

"For example, some leaders at Ford were persuaded that buying a luxury brand like Jaguar was required to enhance the Ford image. So, Ford invested billions in the purchase of Jaguar at the urging of brand managers. Then they invested billions more to revamp the product, restructure the organization, modernize the assembly plant operations and market it. When evaluating the profitability of Jaguar, our company's analysts virtually ignored the original capital investment and associated expenses. Unrelated incentives allowed executives involved to be rewarded while the Jaguar part of the company lost a fortune.

"Can you imagine Ford selling around 35,000 Jaguars per year with billions invested? Trying to make a profit with billions invested, very few dealers and only 35,000 thousand units in sales for the entire U.S., is practically impossible. But the brand managers wanted to keep only a select few dealers, insisting that the formula for profitable growth was to keep this premium luxury brand very limited and exclusive. This strategy led to huge financial losses," finished Christopher, showing his exasperation.

"Drawing from our previous conversations, it seems that if profitability was the benchmark used for performance reviews and compensation of managers, their first priority would be to get more franchised dealers in the U.S. and sell more product," Mr. Carman declared. "They must understand that profitability is defined as revenue minus cost."

Christopher paused and drew a deep breath. He was always surprised by how well Mr. Carman could drive home a point.

"You cannot ignore initial capital investment and related expenses!" Mr. Carman nearly roared. Color was returning to his cheeks now, even before the soybean tea had been served.

"Exactly!" Christopher exclaimed. "Aston Martin does well in James Bond movies, but as a business model in our portfolio, it's terrible. It's another example of a very poor business acquisition. The simple truth is that brand management brings very little to the bottom line. At Ford, it just creates a place where snake oil salesmen, disguised as brand management consultants, can hide and be overcompensated.

"Brand management is supposedly the application of marketing techniques to a specific product, product line, or brand," Christopher explained. "It seeks to increase the product's perceived value to the customer, thereby increasing brand franchise and brand equity. However, branding should never upstage common sense. Much of the advice from brand managers hasn't worked. For instance, it was so-called brand management consultants who convinced Ford decision makers to eliminate the iconic Ford Oval."

Christopher continued. "At the time, the Blue Oval was the second most recognizable brand symbol in the world. My son, at the age of four, understood the significance of the Ford Oval, and everywhere he saw it, he would say, 'That is the company my daddy works for!' But, in the name of brand management, Ford developed the scripted Ford Motor Company logo, even though the Ford Oval was the face of the brand for decades. These so-called experts convinced Ford management that the Ford Oval limited the brand. The new scripted logo was supposedly more sophisticated in their minds and would allow marketing of these other premium brands like Jaguar, Aston Martin, Volvo and Land Rover under it. All this so they could create something new they could take credit and get paid for."

"Well, how did that go over?" Mr. Carman asked.

"Of course, the change in the logo failed miserably," Christopher replied. "Nobody seemed to take into account that we had spent billions of dollars and decades building equity in the original Ford logo and that it would take billions of dollars to duplicate the recognition we had already gained with the Ford brand. Disregarding the studies that showed the Ford Oval was the second most recognized corporate symbol in the world, overnight those brand managers threw it out like yesterday's leftovers and tried to create this new thing. I hate to sound like an alarmist, but this was a very serious mistake."

Mr. Carman interrupted him, breaking into a little grin.

"You know what Will Rogers would say about all this brand management?"

"What?" Christopher asked, falling right into Mr. Carman's humor trap.

"He would say that 'nothing you can't spell will ever work.'" Christopher shook his head and smiled at the simple truth in Will Rogers' humor and he continued on.

"Following the advice of the brand management gurus, Ford management also dropped nameplates like Escort and Taurus. The experts said that product names not beginning with 'F' for the Ford line, 'M' for Mercury, and 'E' for SUVs, were inconsistent with the preferred brand image. The problem with that thinking was that it ignored the billions of dollars already spent to build the Escort and Taurus brands. Both models were for many years the best-selling vehicles in the world! To create and launch a new brand in the minds of consumers costs billions. This capital-intensive marketing strategy also failed. Both replacement products for the Escort and Taurus — the original Focus and the Five Hundred — have produced less than half the sales of their predecessors. This is the kind of thinking and marketing that led to many years of declining sales and market share."

"Indeed," said Mr. Carman.

"I don't understand how the company could invest billions in brands like Escort and Taurus for over 20 years and then walk away," said Christopher, clearly frustrated. "We must retain those strong nameplates that have built up so much equity and customer loyalty. Think of the time, energy, and brainpower wasted coming to the conclusion that all of the Ford brand names must start with the letter 'F'. All that time and energy would have been much better invested in developing a car that people wanted to buy.

"I know this may seem trivial," Christopher continued, "but when you are trying to improve your car line-up and you yank out one of the props supporting your sales like nameplate recognition, that's poor judgment. Heck, the Taurus was the top-selling car in America from 1992 to 1996. We have a bad habit of trying to launch new names to revive tarnished brands rather than sticking with the good names and improving the vehicles."

"Has Ford decided that recognized product names have no meaning or value?" asked Mr. Carman. "They shouldn't be thrown away like old shoes."

Christopher was glad to hear that Mr. Carman understood his concerns. *Are they going to change the 'Mustang' name next? There must be a way to alert upper management to the fact that nobody outside of the brand management offices thinks it's a neat idea to have every car name start with the same initial as the name of the company. Surely our new boss, Mulally, won't tolerate any of this silly stuff. He's got a company to save,* he thought to himself.

Christopher continued with some encouraging news. "The Taurus is coming back into the lineup at Ford. When Mulally arrived, one of the first things he did was ask a very poignant question: *What happened to the Taurus?* The simple and obvious prodding was meant to be a subtle wakeup call to current management. How could Ford be so foolish to kill a strong nameplate like Taurus? It's now official; the Taurus name will be back temporarily on a rebadged Ford Five Hundred until the all-new

Taurus is developed. Clear evidence that Ford has made a serious commitment to reinventing the Taurus as a first-class four-door sedan.

"Ironically, brand management eventually led Ford down a path of consistently communicating the wrong message to the wrong group of consumers," explained Christopher. "These consultants, some of whom were paid millions to come up with a new brand idea, were ignoring the most basic principles of marketing. An example is the implementation of another 'beauty' of an idea called the 'Bold Moves' advertising campaign, where advertising focused on telling silly stories and showing a Ford Edge driving on the side of a skyscraper. In most cases, the products can speak for themselves without brand managers having to create crazy advertising schemes.

"Another message we tried to communicate was 'Lincoln Represents American Luxury.' Well, that's good, but they defined the market segment incorrectly because they based it on their mystical research. They began marketing to a consumer group that couldn't even afford to buy luxury cars. Then, they did the same with Mercury. They developed the idea that 'Mercury Is Metro-Cool,' and defined that by what they thought 'Metro-Cool' was. When they listed the characteristics of the individuals that 'Metro-Cool' would appeal to, they were not our loyal customer base. They were not a group of people who paid their bills on time, were respected in the community, went to church on Sunday, or were active in helping others. They seemed to purposely avoid marketing to the salt of the earth, basically good people that had historically been our bread and butter loyal customers. Brand management consultants convinced us that the hardworking American public — the same people who have been buying Fords for generations — were not who we want to buy future Fords because they weren't cool enough."

"Why, hard-working, average Americans are exactly who Ford *should* be marketing to," Mr. Carman pronounced. "What in the world could be wrong with that?"

"I remember raising my hand in a meeting after a presentation by brand managers on what they thought should be our new target consumer groups," Christopher reminisced. "I tried to remind these brand managers that it is Ford who owns the credit company that is financing these Metro-Cool consumers who are overextended, impulse buyers with a history of not paying their bills. It is Ford that would be taking enormous risks to ensure that the cool consumers are the ones driving Fords. I stated that we were forsaking the basic ideals our company was founded on. All of this in the name of brand management!"

"Well, what did they say to that?" Mr. Carman wondered aloud.

"The brand management experts looked at me and said, 'we are trying to align the Ford brand with the people who are cool, like dot-com and computer geeks, even if they overextended themselves.' They said, 'Times change and we must too.'"

"Times change?" Mr. Carman asked. "What is that for an answer on why Ford should turn away from the very consumers who made the company what it is today?"

"Not to mention that overextending yourself when you are in a credit game will only make you have a bad book of business which will cost big money," added Christopher. "Having to continuously write off bad debt will cause your credit rating to go down, limiting credit to creditworthy consumers. But Ford's senior management was so bewitched by brand management that they were suckered in again."

"How can this be?" asked an exasperated Mr. Carman.

"Well, some of these brand managers are pretty savvy," he explained. "They study brand management or get their MBA and suddenly become brand management experts with no real industry experience to build upon. They don't want to build on a company's existing brand because that would not be sexy or get them the credit or payoff. Then, when they want to do something that is different from what makes good sense, they start with their mantra, 'The brand would dictate that we do this,' or 'the brand DNA would suggest that.' It's just like astrology; if you write it vaguely enough, anything could relate to the desired brand DNA. What's more, they intimidate managers or leaders who question the changes by acting like they don't understand brand management.

"So, that's what happened," concluded Christopher. "The science of astrological brand management led us to sponsor events that missed our target market, launch expensive campaigns, and do countless other things all to supposedly 'line up with the brand.' For example, Ford spent millions endorsing a professional golfer on the PGA Tour, but was that really money well spent? When you look at the interests of typical Ford customers, we would have been much wiser to spend just a fraction of that money targeting the outdoor crowd of over 60 million hunters and fisherman."

Christopher paused. "That reminds me of an enormous opportunity we continue to miss the mark on. Ford has a golden opportunity to capture and dominate mind share in the truck market, with one of the most brand loyal consumer groups in the industry — the American Sportsman. But in order to turn mind share into market share gains, we need to craft and deliver a truly authentic message that speaks 'lifestyle' to this very large group of environmental and conservation-minded consumers. Can you imagine a specialty edition truck designed specifically for the American Sportsman? We've delivered specialty trucks better than anyone over the years with examples like King Ranch and Harley Davidson. How about a Mossy Oak Edition Ford Truck?"

"Mossy Oak, what's Mossy Oak," inquired Mr. Carman.

"They're a licensing company and a real big-time brand in the outdoor world," answered Christopher. "Guess I better leave that idea with the marketing folks though, I've got my hands full as it is.

"What brand management seems to do is allow these consultants to bring in friends of theirs — cronies who are so-called brand experts and advertising executives — and overpay them with no accountability for the actual impact on sales. If they were paid for results, they would have had to return millions to Ford, instead of taking home their millions in compensation."

"Unbelievable!" said Mr. Carman. "All the while, Ford is paying for this foolishness?"

"You see, consultants prey on this science of brand management. They hover around like scavengers who come in and offer you brand management advice for millions of dollars that never justifies itself in vehicle sales gains. Ford was sold snake oil."

"Well, as I said, we had snake oil salesmen in my day, too," Mr. Carman said. "Every week, they would come in promising that if we would use their motor oil, the engine would never wear out, or if we would use their fuel, we could double or triple the fuel efficiency of our vehicles. The fact is, no product existed that could do any of those things and we knew it. I guess they didn't learn, did they? Yeah, we had brand managers in my time — I've met those guys before. We ran them out of the company once, and it sounds like that needs to happen again.

"You know," Mr. Carman continued. "Ford Motor Company was built on the foundation of maximizing profits through the establishment of mass production systems and intellectual property rights. Ford challenged the business model of others who were focused only on inventing premium vehicles for the rich. A good friend of mine once said that he wouldn't want to invent anything that wouldn't sell, and I agree. 'Sales are proof of utility and utility is success,' my friend always said. A misconception by many is that the money value of an invention constitutes the reward to its inventor. But I always found my greatest pleasure, and so my reward, in the work that preceded what the world calls success, because I enjoyed the work itself more than the reward. I never did anything by accident, nor did any of my inventions for the company come by accident — they came by work. Another thing I've learned is that success does not bring happiness, but rather, happiness brings success. The three great essentials to achieving anything worthwhile are hard work, dedication, and common sense. Remember to remind them, Christopher, that bad alliances and bad ideas mathematically equal waste, and waste is worse than loss. The scope of thrift is limitless."

At that very moment, the grandfather clock chimed seven times. Christopher had not worn a watch today. He had taken it back to the shop to be repaired. *They really should fix that old clock*, he thought to himself.

Mr. Carman stood up and glanced thoughtfully at the old grandfather clock. His cough began to act up again. The room became cold and damp and the lights flickered. It was time to go.

"Mr. Carman," Christopher said, standing up to leave, "Thank you for hearing me out and listening to my views on brand management and the detriment it has been to Ford. I don't know why, but I can't help feeling like you really understand what we are going through. I have this feeling that you will be able to help us."

Mr. Carman smiled patiently and walked with him to the entrance. Christopher grabbed his coat from the cloakroom. Mr. Carman waved good-bye and said, "I'll see you tomorrow, then, same time, same place."

"Develop and foster an environment that encourages truth tellers." — *Mr. Carman*

CHAPTER TEN

OVER-ENGINEERED

*"If everyone is moving forward together, then success takes care
of itself." — Henry Ford*

THE NEXT DAY, when Christopher arrived at Fairlane Manor to meet with Mr. Carman, he noticed yet another antique car parked in front of the estate. This time, Mr. Carman was in the driver's seat, and Christopher could see the silhouette of someone seated next to him. Christopher pulled up in front of the Model T and called out to Mr. Carman.

"Wow, just how many of these little collectibles do you have?" he asked. "This one looks brand new!"

"It's pretty new, Christopher!" Mr. Carman replied. "I thought that today, since the weather is a bit better, we might ride around the grounds. Albert has even prepared us a picnic lunch. I also invited an old friend of mine to join in our conversation today, and I thought it appropriate for old times' sake, that we eat outdoors. My friend and I used to go on camping trips together. Great fun it was — building dams on small streams and examining old mills for a calculation of the power output!" Mr. Carman recollected.

Christopher was always amazed by Mr. Carman's vast variety of interests. He had noticed that the weather today was somewhat better. Sunlight had broken through the dark clouds which seemed to hover over Fairlane Manor lately, and the warm rays were burning off some patches of fog. *It would be nice to enjoy the afternoon outside*, he thought.

"Well, you know what they say," Christopher laughed.

"There are only two seasons in Michigan — winter and the Fourth of July! I guess today is more like the Fourth of July! We should enjoy the weather while we can." Christopher could see that the man in the passenger's seat was laughing with Mr. Carman at his joke. The man gave him a friendly wave.

"Nice to meet you, sir," said Christopher.

The man didn't seem to hear him.

"Speak up, Christopher. Talk right into his ear if you can," Mr. Carman directed. "He's been hard of hearing for years!"

Mr. Carman smiled.

Christopher leaned forward toward the man. "Nice to meet you, sir," he called out more loudly this time. The man turned around and returned the smile.

"It's a pleasure to meet you too," he replied.

Christopher didn't know his name nor did he venture to ask. Besides, if Mr. Carman had wanted him to know it, he would have told him. Mr. Carman was a man of many peculiar confidences, he had learned.

"Park your vehicle and hop on in, young man," Mr. Carman called to Christopher, who pulled next to him. Mr. Carman's mood today was playful. Being in the company of his old friend seemed to help him forget his worries and his nagging cough. He was bundled up for the outdoors, wearing a heavy woolen scarf wrapped securely around his neck to keep him extra warm.

Christopher studied the man in the passenger seat of the car as they drove along the garden roads of Fairlane Manor. He was a distinguished-looking gentleman. He wore a three-piece vested suit. A perky black bow tie sat neatly atop his white starched, round-collared shirt, and gold initialed cufflinks peeked out of his coat sleeves. *Maybe these guys are members of an antique car club of sorts*, he thought.

Mr. Carman's friend had a mass of snowy-white hair which was combed to the side of his high forehead. He had an air of high class and wit about him. As he turned around, Christopher saw his bushy dark eyebrows framing ice blue eyes full of fire and passion. The man sat contentedly beside his friend, looking out at the countryside, enjoying the ride as Mr. Carman drove his car down the winding roads of the estate.

They arrived at a small pond. There, next to a field of what looked like newly planted vegetables, were a table and chairs carved in stone. The table was set, and plates of food were already waiting for them. Christopher recognized the familiar steam rising from the cups of tea. He watched as Mr. Carman walked over to his friend and put his arm around his shoulder. The two men began to reminisce about their past.

"Remember the convention in Manhattan Beach?" asked Mr. Carman.

"Why, of course I do," his friend answered. "Yes, it was quite a banquet."

"And do you remember the time we first met? You marveled at our self-contained car that carried its own power plant. Why, you banged your fist down on the table, ecstatic about that gas car we made!" recounted Mr. Carman.

His friend let out a jolly laugh.

"That bang on the table was worth the world to me," continued Mr. Carman. "No man up to then had given me any encouragement. I had hoped that I was headed in the right direction. Sometimes I knew that I was, sometimes I only wondered, but here, all at once and out of the clear blue, the greatest inventive genius in the world — you — had given me complete approval. I will never forget that."

The man smiled warmly at Mr. Carman.

"And do you remember the crowds which lined 30 miles of Detroit streets on the 50th anniversary party for the institute?" reminded the man. "Your company sent in seven railroad cars of New Jersey soil for the re-enactment of my company's first successful invention in our laboratories."

Mr. Carman nodded and smiled.

"You even tried to get an old elm tree that stood near the lab door, but had to settle for planting one in the same spot," added the man. The two men chuckled and laughed as Christopher stood to the side, leaning on the hood of the Model T. He wanted to leave the two buddies alone and not to appear to be eavesdropping on their conversation. It seemed to be a very special moment for Mr. Carman, and he was happy for him.

"The whole nation turned their lights on that night — in honor of the anniversary celebration," remarked Mr. Carman.

"They sure did," replied the man.

As the two men spoke together, the warm light of memory surrounded them. Mr. Carman seemed years younger today. Their energy was electrifying. Mr. Carman's friend took a cigar out of his vest pocket, lit it and puffed away. Mr. Carman took sips of his favorite drink, soybean tea. The mood was light and peaceful.

Christopher had stepped into a world where the line between dreams and reality, fiction and nonfiction coincided. He felt like he was walking on a moving ramp toward a light at the end of a long dark tunnel.

Albert arrived with a fresh pot of tea, and they all sat down at the picnic table for lunch. Christopher sat on the cold stone bench. He placed his pen and notepad on the table, ready to write. They got down to business as Mr. Carman introduced the conversation of the day.

"Engineering is one of the most exciting and important functions of any manufacturing company. Why, without engineering, realizing an inventor's creation would be impossible," Mr. Carman remarked. His friend nodded in agreement.

"See that automobile over there?" Mr. Carman continued. "The Model T was one of the most important and successful automobiles ever engineered. Christopher, did you know that the Model T was the chief instrument of one of the greatest and most rapid changes in the lives of the common people in history, and that it affected this dramatic change in less than two decades?"

Christopher smiled. He had never thought of it that way before.

"After the Model T came along, farmers were no longer isolated on remote farms," Mr. Carman explained. "Reliance on horses for transportation disappeared so rapidly that the transfer of acreage from hay to other crops caused an agricultural revolution. In turn, the automobile became the main prop of the American economy and a stimulant to urbanization. Cities spread outward, creating suburbs and housing developments. Soon came the building of the finest highway system in the world. The original Ford cars were built for the great multitude. The car was made to be the ordinary man's utility rather than the rich man's luxury, so millions could go wherever they pleased."

"That was part of Henry Ford's vision and what transitioned our society from the agricultural era to the industrial era," Christopher contributed. Mr. Carman's friend listened intently, nodding his head in agreement.

"In my engineering days," Mr. Carman recalled, "I was always of the mentality of not merely achieving increased capacity, but complete self-sufficiency. The making of the Model T is a great example of this. World War I had many shortages and price increases which demonstrated the need to control raw materials. Wheels, tires, upholstery, and a number of accessories were purchased from other suppliers. As Model T production increased, these smaller operations had to speed their output, and many had to install their own assembly lines. It had become impossible to coordinate production and shipment so that each product would arrive at the right place and at the right time. At first, the company tried accumulating large inventories to prevent delays or stoppages of the assembly line. They soon realized that stockpiling was wasted capital. At that time, it was thought that manufacturing began the moment raw material was separated from the earth and continued until the finished product was delivered to the consumer.

"The company built a plant in River Rouge that embodied the idea of an integrated operation, encompassing production, assembly, and transportation. In pursuit of a true vertical integration model, the company purchased a railroad, acquired control of 16 coal mines and about 700,000 acres of timberland. They also built a sawmill, acquired a fleet of Great Lakes freighters to bring ore from Lake Superior mines, and bought a glassworks as well. Imagine that!

"The move from Highland Park to the completed River Rouge plant was accomplished in 1927," Mr. Carman reflected. "At eight o'clock every morning, just enough ore for the day would arrive on a Ford freighter from Ford mines in Michigan and Minnesota and would be transferred by conveyor to the blast furnaces. Then, it was transformed into steel with heat supplied by coal from Ford mines in Kentucky. It would continue on through the foundry molds and stamping mills until, exactly twenty-eight hours after its arrival as ore, the material would emerge as a finished automobile. Similar systems handled lumber for floorboards, rubber for tires, and so on. At the height of its success, the company's holdings stretched from the iron mines of northern Michigan to the jungles of Brazil and across 33 countries around the globe. Most remarkably, not one cent had been borrowed to pay for any of it. It was all built out of profits from the Model T."

"That's amazing," Christopher said. "We forget how incredibly integrated Ford's manufacturing process was at the time."

"Back to Ford Motor Company today," Mr. Carman continued. "How is the company optimizing its engineering capabilities? After all, Ford's engineering rests on a foundation of almost a century of solid technical and business experience."

"Well," Christopher began, caught a little off guard. "There's one specific solution for the engineering problems facing Ford today, and that is to build all vehicles worldwide to U.S. standards and not sign a contract with the union that restricts the company from importing and exporting freely."

"That sounds sensible," Mr. Carman commented. "Do you see any other opportunities for improvement?"

"Well, we haven't maximized economies of scale to the fullest extent like we should if we were truly looking at the global picture and putting it all in perspective," replied Christopher.

"In recent years, it seems we've allowed each engineering team, each vehicle team, each commodity team, and each platform team to optimize their vehicle independent of others in style and in part content. Each product is then designed and built without regard to other product lines, and in the end, that just doesn't work. There has to be accountability upward and somebody who says, 'You can optimize your vehicle, but here's the menu to choose from.' Without this accountability, we've over-engineered many of our products, which cost us millions of dollars in lost economies of scale. As a result, we have dozens of different alternators and starters when we really only need a few, and we have just as many steering wheels, when Toyota has just a handful."

"Is that so?" Mr. Carman asked thoughtfully. "It seems the company needs to focus on engineering efficiency."

Christopher commented, "allowing engineers creative freedom to create whatever they want may work on cable TV reality shows like *Pimp My Ride* or *West Coast Choppers*, but it's a recipe for disaster in the automobile assembly business. You must manage your costs and improve the serviceability. I always think the vehicles on those shows are so cool, but you never see what happens when those one-of-a-kind gadgets go bad or break down. And, most people could never afford to buy one like that."

"Pimp my ride?" asked Mr. Carman, bewildered.

Mr. Carman's friend also seemed perplexed.

"They used to be popular reality TV shows," Christopher replied, but by the confused look on the gentlemen's faces, Christopher surmised that neither was familiar with them. Explaining that further might take the conversation off track when time was of the essence. He decided to leave it at that.

"As I see it," Christopher continued. "There's too much complexity, and this limits our economies of scale in purchasing and makes serviceability a nightmare. Dealers have to stock too many parts in order to service vehicles or risk causing customer delays for vehicle repairs if the parts are not in stock."

Mr. Carman's friend turned to them and suggested, "the engineering departments must share best practices or lessons learned with other teams. Everyone should be aiming for the same goal, which is making the best products possible. Sharing information within the company is the best way to achieve that. Don't they know that TEAM stands for Together Everyone Achieves More?" the man exclaimed.

"Seems today, there's simply too much engineering in the engineering department," explained Christopher "Too many are self-serving, trying to maximize their own careers. The mentality is, 'If I come with the best product, and it's really cool, then I'll be in line for the next promotion.' That could be solved with a restructuring of compensation that provides incentives for team sharing and a focus on shared platforms and economies of scale.

"Too many engineers want to go with the latest technology, sometimes before it's adequately tested. And since parts are not uniform across all the products, a Ford customer may get in one product and the gas tank is on the left side when in the next product, it's on the right. We probably have 40 different gas tanks. Our products should have a consistent feel throughout every shared platform."

Mr. Carman shook his head and seemed astonished at the numbers Christopher was spouting.

"In order for Ford to truly thrive," Christopher continued. "We have to have more commonly shared platforms and common parts so we can buy at a discounted rate using economies of scale. Toyota and Honda have been doing this for years. They actually continue using the same platforms as they update a model from year to year and simply tweak it as new, tested technology becomes available. In other words, if it's working, they don't break it. When you get inside a Toyota or Honda, it's simple and consistent. They also keep their cost structure down because they are using the same parts in multiple vehicles.

"Ford seems to look at it the other way around; if it isn't broke, break it. They redo entire models with new parts, which cost a lot and makes it harder to service. This whole engineering problem creates issues in mass parts production and dealer complexity in servicing the vehicles anywhere in the world. With more accountability from the engineering departments for quality problems or lost profits, I don't think we'd have so much variability and complexity," suggested Christopher.

"I'd think not," agreed Mr. Carman.

"Another problem in engineering is in the use of U.S. standards for our vehicles," Christopher explained. "Ford builds North American products to U.S. standards and builds all other products to meet the local standards in the countries they're produced in. Toyota builds to U.S. standards all across the world so they can move their products around. So, if a Ford product is successful in another part of the world, we can't bring it in to the U.S. because the costs to bring it up to U.S. standards retroactively would be prohibitive. If we built U.S. standards into the costs when originally manufacturing all of our products, the cost difference would be insignificant and we could transfer successful products across all markets. Economies of scale would easily offset standardization.

"One significant reason we don't transfer successful products from other countries into the U.S. is the United Auto Workers, one of the most powerful unions in the country. They will fight it tooth and nail. We brought in a car called the Merkur several years ago. It was a German car. The UAW went crazy. We have the KA in Europe, which is a dynamite sub-compact car. We could use it here in America, as an entry-level small car that we badly need. We already have it designed in Europe. It's ready to go, but we can't bring it to the U.S. because the UAW would probably threaten to walk out. They would walk off the lines and shut the company down. And, you guessed it — the KA is not engineered to U.S. standards anyway. So, to develop the KA in the U.S., we have to get on our three- or four-year product development cycle to design and build a separate North American version costing billions."

"Let me get this straight, son," said Mr. Carman, trying to digest all that Christopher was saying. "From what you're telling me, Ford currently has no current global platform built to U.S. standards and little accountability installed in the engineering department. This is all critical to long term profitablity. Leadership has to *lead*. This whole mess sounds like mutiny on the high seas!"

"Thank goodness our new leadership team and the engineering 'top boss' are making the necessary changes that will lead to major improvement in this area. There are strong rumors of European small cars coming to North America in the 2010 calendar year," Christopher replied.

"As your friend wisely said, there needs to be a sharing of ideas too. There needs to be collaboration and cooperation. Our engineers have to be rewarded for being team players, not lone rangers.

"Here is a hypothetical example: the industry standard for engineering a certain vehicle might be eight out of ten. But, if an engineer is full of himself and full of his future with Ford, he might decide that, for the vehicle he is working on, the standard is going to be a nine. Even though every vehicle in the world is built to an eight standard, because of Ford's engineering practices, this engineer can arbitrarily decide that it's going to be a nine. This decision instantly negates using any common platforms or any common parts. Special parts have to be developed which meet the Ford spec, which is already above everything else. And so, as a result of this unnecessary over-engineering, Ford prices itself out of the market. The eight standard requires a five dollar part, but the nine standard requires a seven dollar part. Those costs must be built in to the price. A vehicle is made up of about 15,000 parts on average. The parts are made from a variety of plastics, metals, and even space-age materials. The parts go through a rigorous production process where they are bonded, welded, screwed, and riveted together. Then, when the production process is complete, the parts have to be able to work in temperatures below freezing and above 100 degrees.

"Without engineering commonality into this process, there is no discipline and you can see where costs can run amok quickly," continued

Christopher. "If our manufacturing process is 90 percent accurate, there is still a potential failure of 150 parts. Even if we are 99.9 percent accurate, there is still a potential failure of 15 parts. That is why engineering is critical to achieving best in class quality."

Mr. Carman was visibly disturbed by what Christopher had shared with him. He fidgeted around in his chair and tried to keep from coughing. Albert appeared and brought the group more soybean tea. Mr. Carman's friend frowned and shook his head from side to side.

"The best example of this," continued Christopher, "is the Ford Contour and Mercury Mystique, which inside the company we called the Ford 'mistake.' They tried to force a new segment that was somewhere between an Escort and a Taurus, but that cost more than a Taurus. It was an over-engineered product that should have cost a billion dollars to produce, but instead it cost several billion! Employees who were on these teams were rewarded and promoted instead of being held accountable for the cost overage. They essentially built the Edsel — a product that nobody wanted. The Escort and Taurus were very highly successful vehicles leading their segments at that time — among the top five sellers in the world. Imagine trying to create a product between two of the top five sellers in the world that was going to cost more than either of them.

"Also, Ford consistently let good products go stale," he continued. "Toyota is the best at avoiding this trap. The Toyota refreshing process is a great example of using the correct engineering perspective. Their strategy is to refresh the product and keep tweaking it so that you can differentiate between model years. They have a continuous process of refreshing their products as opposed to Ford's process, which is based on totally re-engineering the entire product every several years. We reengineer the power train, the suspension, put in new technology, and reengineer it from one end to the other. Replacing the Escort and Taurus, which were great cars of premium quality, was crazy."

"Why would anyone try to reinvent a product that was already selling so well?" Mr. Carman questioned.

"I certainly don't know!" Christopher replied. It was a relief for him to speak with someone who really listened and seemed to understand. He felt as if a huge weight had been lifted off his shoulders. As he spoke, his heart felt lighter and he was hopeful, just having someone with whom he could share these concerns.

Mr. Carman turned to his friend.

"Tell me, my friend, what do you make of all this?" asked Mr. Carman.

The man leaned forward, took another puff from his cigar, and said: "In my days, my engineering team was persistent in their efforts to design and produce a successful product that would be profitable, useful, reliable, cost-effective, and could improve the quality of people's lives. We could have made thousands of different light bulbs, but what if they all had ended up being defective? Would this invention have survived to the 21st century as it has? Engineering with very little accountability and without an overall plan is irresponsible. We strived to make one excellent product that would out-do all others and stand the test of time. Products should also be strategically designed for compatibility, product evolution and be able to easily integrate into other platforms and systems.

"For example, our engineering team had developed a version of the light bulb that was able to outstrip the other prototypes of inventors at the time, because of a combination of factors. We had an effective incandescent material, a higher vacuum than others were able to achieve, and a high-resistance lamp that made power distribution from a centralized source economically viable. Those factors made us successful in inventing an entire, integrated system of electric lighting. Engineering was the key to our competitive advantage.

"Let me share with you some lessons I've learned along the way. Remember that genius is one percent inspiration, and 99 percent perspiration. Also remember that just because something doesn't do what you planned it to do, doesn't mean it's useless. Finally, remember that many of life's failures are from people who did not realize how close they were to success when they gave up. Last but not least, be courageous! Whatever setback America has encountered, it has always emerged as a stronger and more prosperous nation."

"Thank you for sharing your experience and wisdom with me," said Christopher. "You can't imagine how helpful our conversation today has been. I can't believe you actually worked with the engineers that created one of the most important inventions in the history of the world — the light bulb! You must have been very close to Mr. Edison?"

The man nodded.

"Sure was…heck of a guy!"

Mr. Carman and his friend chuckled.

Christopher had recalled seeing photos of Mr. Edison at the Henry Ford Museum only a few days ago, and this man's resemblance to Edison was remarkable. *Perhaps these old guys were so enamored by these great inventors that they actually emulated them in appearance and style,* he thought. But even that rationalization didn't quite cut it, as it all seemed so real.

Christopher looked at the two men before him. It was a moment he would never forget and a day he would always remember. He looked across the fields far into the valley beyond. He felt proud to be a Ford man and to be an American. For a second, his thoughts drifted off into his own past. He remembered reciting his Boy Scout pledge, the Pledge of Allegiance to the Flag, the Lord's Prayer, and the Golden Rule. Christopher was thankful that such rituals had helped shape his life.

The sun stayed out until the three companions reached the main house. Then it began to rain. He was lost in his thoughts for a few moments and didn't see Mr. Carman's friend leave. A melancholy mood had now moved in, and Mr. Carman seemed weary as his cough began to act up again.

"Tomorrow, same time, same place?" Christopher asked gently.

Mr. Carman nodded.

"Make common sense common practice." — *Mr. Carman*

CHAPTER NINE

DIVERSITY

"'Who ought to be boss?' is like
'who ought to be the tenor in the quartet?'
Obviously the man who can sing tenor."
— Henry Ford

T HE WEEK FLEW by, and there were only a few days left before the 60th anniversary of the passing of Henry Ford. Christopher had spent the early part of the morning on the phone with Frank McIntyre. The two had been discussing one of the more controversial subjects Frank was addressing in his article — diversity policies within corporate America. Even though Frank was a trusted colleague, Christopher still felt tense discussing the subject with him. He had been mindful to address the subject carefully. In fact, Frank had offered a few pointed questions that Christopher had requested they come back to later in the day. He planned to have his meeting with Mr. Carman before tackling Frank's toughest questions, anticipating that Mr. Carman could offer helpful insights into Ford's take on dealing with diversity and discrimination in the politically correct environment of today.

Christopher thought he would get to Fairlane Manor a little earlier than usual to prepare his thoughts. Heading down the hallway to the elevator, he noticed Joy walking toward him, holding a paper in her hand. Her expression was tense.

"I'm glad I caught you before you left. Wait 'til you read this!" she exclaimed. "It just came in over the wire."

Christopher glanced over the AP wire, then looked up at Joy, who was anxiously waiting for his reaction to the news.

"Please give word that no one is to speak with the press — no emails, calls, nothing for now," he directed.

"Why don't you go ahead and schedule a department meeting with everyone this afternoon for three o'clock? I'll be back by then. And don't worry, Joy, everything will work out fine."

"Sure thing. Thanks, Mr. Hope." He folded the newswire and put it in his jacket pocket. It was more bad news for Ford and pointed to more tough times ahead. He was so grateful to have Mr. Carman to talk to.

As it had since his first meeting with Mr. Carman, the weather seemed to change as he approached Fairlane Manor. Clouds would suddenly appear and fog would begin to creep over the fields and roads. Christopher wasn't sure what to make of it. He struggled to keep his focus on the tasks at hand and the incredible opportunity to speak with someone who had been there and seen it all. Mr. Carman, along with his friend's wise advice and his instinctive, uncanny ability to draw out from Christopher the unfiltered truth about what was really going on at Ford, was unique and remarkable. Mr. Carman was different from anyone Christopher had ever met before — a voice from the past with a very clear vision for the future.

When he pulled up to the gates of the manor, he could not believe his eyes. Crowds of elegantly dressed ladies wearing pearls, feathered hats and furs, and gentlemen in formal wear and top hats were gathered around a parade of 10 of the most beautiful antique Ford cars he had ever seen. They were laughing and walking around the cars, admiring them and chatting it up. Albert and a team of servants were moving about offering beverages and trays of snacks. There were also more plainly dressed folks wearing overalls, and he guessed they were local farmers, workers, and car mechanics. He had never seen anything like it before. It was all unfolding like a dream in slow motion.

This must be a film, he thought to himself, but there were no cameras in sight. *Or maybe it's an auto collectors' club party.*

The parking attendant came running out to greet Christopher.

"What's happening here today?" Christopher asked.

"It's a parade of Mr. Carman's finest automobiles," the attendant exclaimed.

"Who are all these people?" asked Christopher. "Are they filming a movie or something?"

The attendant didn't have time to answer him. Mr. Carman was waving to him from the porch of the manor, motioning for him to come join him. As the attendant left to park his car, he approached the crowd, excusing himself as he elbowed his way through. Before he got to the front porch, he stopped and admired the lineup of Mr. Carman's antique cars. They were all spectacular.

"Just in time for lunch, young man," said Mr. Carman when he was within shouting distance. "What's the occasion for the parade today?" Christopher pressed, hoping for a rational explanation.

"There's no occasion needed to spend a day admiring the work of American auto workers," replied Mr. Carman.

As they walked into the entrance of the manor, Christopher turned around to take one last look at the crowd gathered on the front lawn. But when he did, he didn't know what to think. Everyone had vanished. Not one person in sight. All of the beautiful antique cars had disappeared too. It seemed impossible for everyone to have left so fast and for all the cars to have been driven away. There had been no sound of engines, only a light rain tapping.

Mr. Carman was already several paces ahead of him. As he followed Mr. Carman up the steps toward the entrance, Fairlane Manor's timekeeper chimed seven times. Christopher counted each one as he walked toward the dining room. The fire was ablaze, and the lunch table was set for three people. He wondered who their guest was today as he saw a man sitting at their table already waiting for them. Albert took Christopher's coat as he walked into the dining hall.

"I've asked someone to join us for lunch. I believe that our topic today will be of great interest to him, and he may lend some insight to one of the most important issues facing the company and America," said Mr. Carman.

He wondered if Mr. Carman had planned on discussing the topic of diversity today. It would be just like him to have known what was on Christopher's mind. Christopher took a closer look at the man seated at the table, a stout black man, impeccably dressed in a gray suit. His mustache was well trimmed and his forehead indented with age lines. The man stood up to greet him, smiling warmly and offering his handshake. He had a tremendous presence and magnetism about him. As usual, Albert brought the cups of soybean tea and lunch began.

Christopher remembered the news release he wanted to show Mr. Carman. "Before we start on our topic today, I have news to share with you," he announced. "I just received this release from the AP wire."

"Ford fell in the sales ranks again and is now considered the fourth largest automobile company in the U.S.," recounted Christopher, visibly shaken by yet another major blow to the company. "GM still has the lead and ranked in first place, followed by Toyota in second, Daimler Chrysler in third, and then Ford in fourth place. For all of my career, actually since 1931, Ford held the number two spot. Toyota passed us several months ago and now Daimler Chrysler has passed us to take the number three slot. This is the first time in all my years with Ford that Daimler Chrysler has outsold us! Is this a sign of the times that Ford is no longer ranked among the Big Three? This is humbling news for Ford."

The three men sat in silence for a few moments. Each seemed to be reflecting in his own thoughts.

Then Mr. Carman spoke.

"Well, Christopher, number four is better than number five," he said. Then, with a gleam in his eye, "what do you say we start plugging up the holes on the sinking ship and get it sailing once again? You know what they say — it ain't over 'til it's over! So, let's begin our topic of today and get on the mend. We've got work to do and very little time to do it."

The other man at the table turned to him and nodded encouragingly.

"Where does Ford stand today on diversity and the issue of discrimination, Christopher?" Mr. Carman's guest beckoned. There was a glow about him, an aura of incredible power. Christopher felt quite safe and comfortable. He then cleared his throat.

"Sir, diversity has gone astray at Ford" Christopher began. "Diversity, in its purest form, is good and allows companies to leverage the opinions and experience of every employee. However, when diversity becomes an initiative or program by itself, it is easy to corrupt the process if it is not managed properly. It can result in an environment where individual members of management can promote their own personal agendas under the umbrella of diversity. What started as a noble effort quickly turned into a quota program. The initial noble effort was hijacked by people who used it to further their own personal interests instead of Ford's. Diversity programs have created dissension. They have become a barrier to teamwork and a great source of inequality, rather than fairness, for the entire workplace. Diversity is an important value, but it can't be more important than creating quality products and getting results."

"You know, it has always been my feeling that no value should be given to things beyond a person's control, such as gender, race, or ethnicity," Mr. Carman stated. "Such things do not guarantee success in business. Focusing on them de-values things that are controllable, like hard work, personal development, and the ability to deliver results. You know, Henry

Ford was the first to pay everyone the same wage for the same job, regardless of race, gender, or ethnicity. Fairness should be an absolute practice for every business and, by definition, should dictate equal treatment for all employees."

The guest raised his eyebrows at Mr. Carman's comment, and spoke up. "My thoughts exactly!" said the man. "I dedicated my life to speaking out against practices of any kind that were based on ethnicity or race alone. True equality is a brotherhood that is color blind, where race is not even an issue. We are all human, one and the same."

Christopher was taken aback by the man's statement. His words were so true, yet painted a much different picture of diversity than Ford's policies seemed to.

"It's refreshing to hear such reasonable views on an issue that has become a distraction at Ford," said Christopher. "I agree that rather than worshiping diversity through artificial programs, Ford should focus on celebrating the uniqueness of every employee. Everyone has uniqueness and should be valued for who they are and how they can contribute to the business. Not everyone is a member of a diverse group, but everyone is unique. Why not treat everyone the same?"

"Everyone *is* unique and everyone *should be* treated the same," exclaimed Mr. Carman. "Why don't you share with us some specific examples of Ford's diversity policies that you feel have gone astray?"

"Well, Ford's diversity policies began as a focus to hire more minority applicants," Christopher explained. "We were advised to pay a premium to hire minority applicants, regardless of their talent and experience in comparison to 'non-diverse' applicants. This hiring quota policy extended to our promotion practices as well. Work group managers were forced to rank all minorities and move some of them above non-diverse performers. Many rode an escalator to the top instead of having to take the stairs.

"In addition, compensation for minorities was higher than for non-diverse employees of the same skillset. It seemed Ford's goal was to look good on paper or in the Ford portrait to the world. Compensation, incentives, and bonuses for minorities became like an entitlement program. As a result, Ford's business agenda was handicapped. Talented employees who had earned promotions were passed over by minority employees. At the same time, many very qualified minority employees already employed at Ford were passed over in favor of bringing in higher profile minority candidates from outside the company.

"It seemed that concerns with public perception and fanfare were prioritized ahead of putting the right person in the right job. As the diversity issue snowballed, minorities in leadership began catering to their own agendas and sought to hire and promote other diverse employees, even if they were not capable of performing their job. Their hiring decisions were not based on qualifications or performance, but rather on ethnicity, race, or gender alone. These factors in hiring decisions fostered discrimination.

"That is why I always preached that discrimination of any kind is intolerable," said Mr. Carman's guest. "Unless you can find a way to be completely color blind when making decisions, true equality cannot be achieved. I always believed that people should be judged by the content of their character, not the color of their skin."

"Equality was certainly not achieved through the diversity initiatives at Ford," said Christopher. "Once, about 10 years ago, at a meeting of the top 100 managers at Ford, a high-ranking manager said in his address, 'I will strike you down if you don't hire and promote people of diversity over white males.' He then required every other manager at Ford to view his speech too. The result was that many talented and proven performers did not perceive a level playing field for them or a future at Ford, so they left our team.

"Then, Ford's diversity mantra evolved to a 'Diversity Is Our Strength' campaign. Diversity became a tool used to promote certain employees at the expense of others and a profitable business model. Ford got into a social reform agenda like the U.S. government, and became much too fond of being politically correct. In the minds of Ford's leadership at the time, diversity became the single most important ingredient to ensure business profitability. There is no doubt that this was one of the first steps causing our poor market position and economic situation because Ford lost focus on developing a performance-driven workforce."

"Diversity of the workforce was always one of Ford's strengths," Mr. Carman interjected. "I think today, the company falsely believes that if they make diversity a primary objective it will somehow guarantee or ensure the profitability of the business model. Well, it never has and never will. Diversity must not be prioritized at the expense of the business model. Diversity should be incorporated as a strength and part of the company's strategy, but not as a goal in and of itself, and certainly not as a guarantee to profitable success without other business policies. Everyone brings something unique to the table, regardless of their race, ethnicity, or gender. Diversity should naturally be one of the strengths of every organization."

"You are right," Christopher continued. "Ironically, Ford talks about increasing diversity in terms of minorities, women, and sexual orientation, but not in terms of diversity of opinions and perspectives. For example, Ford's workplace comes from a narrow geographic base," he explained. "In Ford's U.S. operations, approximately 75 percent of Ford employees come from Michigan or the area within 100 miles of Detroit. The flip side of the coin is that less than seven percent of Ford's vehicles are sold in that market. If Ford were to truly embrace diversity, they would hire, promote, and retain more people from all over the United States. I believe that diversity should include having many perspectives represented, encouraging people to speak their minds, challenge the status quo, and push our company to be more accountable to our shareholders and our customers. Diversity should not simply be about increasing the number of certain types of people."

"What about diversity with regard to age?" Mr. Carman questioned. "Does Ford have the sense to include a vast spectrum of ages in their definition of diversity?"

"Unfortunately, from an experience standpoint, the average age of Ford's workforce is getting younger all the time," Christopher answered. "For years there has been an unspoken policy to get rid of a large number of older employees. It's the 'old white guy' syndrome that supports the idea that older white males are not a desirable part of the workforce. Ford leaders seem to disregard the fact that many of these older white employees have been among our top performers and loyal employees for many, many years. In fact, a former CEO launched a tiered system that purposely disadvantaged older employees, regardless of their contribution. There were even statements made by a number of managers in meetings to the effect that 'this room will look a lot different in the future when some of you old white guys find the door.' As you can imagine, such statements created a very hostile environment. Ford's diversity initiatives seemed to focus on gender, racial, and ethnic diversity as its primary strategy for success, no matter what the cost to overall morale or the financial performance of the company."

"That is outrageous!" Mr. Carman barked. "Human capital is the most important resource any business has. Ford cannot afford to lose any of their great leaders, regardless of their diversity status."

"Diversity is an issue that also concerns the sexual orientation of employees," Christopher added. "Diversity at Ford definitely went wild when the company decided to advertise in homosexual publications and began catering to the homosexual agenda. In doing so, Ford became involved in driving a social agenda that did not relate in the least to profitability.

"Ford's traditional values have always been mainstream and associated with family values. When Ford started championing the gay lifestyle, the American Family Association (AFA) came after us. They were outraged that we were advertising in gay publications and promoting gay sexuality.

This caused a national controversy because our approach was inconsistent with our solid customer base of Americans who champion family values. The debate forced us to take a considerable portion of company resources away from focusing on the business model in order to deal with the uproar caused by a poor decision on advertising."

Christopher continued, "interestingly, however, the AFA did not go after the top six advertisers in gay publications, but only Ford, the seventh top advertiser in these publications. This is another example where some companies get a pass, but the American automobile companies are singled out. A full-fledged boycott followed the AFA's outrage with Ford. Some of our senior managers, in coordination with key dealers, met with the American Family Association (AFA). They made an agreement that when our advertising contracts ran out, they would not be renewed. As soon as they had made this deal, the AFA backed off of their protests and boycotts. There are simply some issues in which Ford as a company should stay out of."

"Ford customers have historically been average, hardworking Americans. If the majority of Ford customers represent one side of an issue, the company shouldn't be involved in promoting the other side so blatantly. Ford must be loyal to its core customers," said Mr. Carman.

"Ford's dealers definitely felt the same way you do," said Christopher. "As a result of the widely publicized reaction of the AFA to our advertising in gay publications, our dealer network went crazy. They were getting complaints from customers who could not believe the family values company they had supported for years would do that. We put our dealers and managers at risk by putting them in the middle of a highly controversial social issue.

"There is little doubt in my mind that this misguided approach to diversity was one of the first steps in the recent erosion of our business," Christopher declared. "Driving personal social agendas on company time, with company money, is misguided and irresponsible. Instead of top performers being promoted accordingly, this so-called diversity agenda began dictating who got promotions and so forth. As Ford's profitability began to suffer due in part to their biased hiring and promotion practices, the luxury of looking the other way and not focusing on key skill-sets of employees or prospective employees could no longer be afforded."

"Incredible!" exclaimed Mr. Carman. "Every company in America and around the world should learn from this."

"Absolutely!" Christopher agreed. "It is a serious case of political correctness gone amok."

Mr. Carman's guest, who had been quite penchant, spoke up abruptly. "Do you know the origin of political correctness?," he asked.

Both Christopher and Mr. Carman nodded 'no'. "It was from Marxist Germany in the 1930's. It was designed to keep people from speaking up about what was going on. It is totally counter to our First Amendment and a dangerous trap to fall into."

"Well," Christopher said. "It is a trap that most American companies and certainly the U.S. government are mired in now." He continued, "what's important to recognize is that Ford was never a non-inclusive work environment in the first place. We treated everyone with respect. The fact that we have had very few discrimination suits supports our history of inclusiveness. Everyone in the company would agree that we need to continue to create and sustain a work environment that allows every employee to be productive without harassment, regardless of their race, gender, or ethnicity."

"Ford shouldn't be driving social agendas at all!" Mr. Carman exclaimed. "Ford's agenda should focus on running a profitable company; they should steer away from social agendas. There's plenty of that going on in the U.S. government."

"I agree," said Christopher. "Our company does our best work when we focus on the business model and on the market ahead."

"That just sounds like common sense to me," Mr. Carman retorted.

"One thing that doesn't relate to common sense at all is the fact that, in the name of diversity, Ford has allowed segmentation of our employees into what are called Employee Resource Groups," Christopher fired back. "These support groups, in fact, create a barrier to unity. Some of these employee groups include the Ford-employee African American Network (FAAN), the Ford Asian-Indian Association (FAIA), the Ford Chinese Association (FCA), the Ford Gay, Lesbian or Bisexual employees (GLOBE), the Ford Hispanic Network Group (FHNG), the Ford Interfaith Network (FIN), the Middle Eastern Community at Ford Motor Company. I might have missed a few, but that's a good number of them," said Christopher.

"It makes me dizzy just trying to remember them all," said Mr. Carman, shaking his head.

"Tell me about it!" said Christopher. "It's a wonder anyone can keep them all straight. I'm not saying that there is anything wrong with having support groups within the company, but we should not take them to the extent that Ford has. These separate groups do more to promote individuality than unity. They force us all to focus on the differences we have rather than what we have in common. We should treat everyone equally instead of taking sides."

"Absolutely!" concurred Mr. Carman. "Finding support from those who share common experiences with you is one thing. But, promotion of social agendas does not belong in the workplace."

Mr. Carman rolled his eyes.

His guest exclaimed: "I don't know whether to laugh or cry. I can't believe what I'm hearing."

"Well, you haven't heard the half of it. I still haven't told you about our Dealer Development program," added Christopher with a sigh. "Originally, Ford's DD program was designed to bring in new dealers — people who had the right skill sets and understood the business, but lacked the resources to start a dealership on their own. Through the DD program,

Ford offered to give these potential dealers financial help and training to get them started. Ford would continue supporting them until they were up and running and able to buy the dealership. The intent was to develop the strength of our dealer network. It was really a great program which allowed many up and coming dealership employees to come in and get a start with Ford's support.

"Unfortunately, it didn't take long for the DD program to turn into a quota-driven program. It became a 'feel good' deal where Ford mainly sought out minorities for the program. Many of the dealers recruited during the quota-driven era of the DD program ended up being some of our least loyal dealers and — needless to say — the least profitable. But, nonetheless, Ford was able to hold its picture perfect diverse head high saying, 'Hey, look how many minority dealers we have and that we support!' Once again, well-intentioned efforts had fallen prey to social agendas. The DD program originally, was in fact, a great program for any dealer candidate needing assistance whether they were a minority or not. Instead, many potentially great dealers missed out on the opportunity and the program still struggles from a profitability standpoint because of Ford's intense focus on diversity being the ultimate priority."

"But you are running a business that's based on profitability — capitalism at its finest, as our country was founded on — not on a social agenda!" interrupted Mr. Carman, markedly agitated. "It's a crying shame that such a program overlooked many qualified potential Ford dealers."

"The DD program costs the company millions each year," Christopher added. "Under this program, not only did Ford recruit minority dealership owners as a rule, but they often replaced a local, experienced dealer with a minority dealership owner who had little or no retail dealership experience. The minority dealers were provided intense training programs to try to make up for their lack of experience.

"Believe it or not, we actually had a mandate that no new dealers would be added anywhere in the country until the minority dealership quota was met. We also ignored geographical considerations. In a sense, we set the new DD dealer up for failure in many instances."

"That's moronic!" exclaimed Mr. Carman.

"How destructive!" Mr. Carman's guest exclaimed.

"Once again, they neglected to look at the reality of the situation," continued Christopher. "We should focus instead on performance-driven candidates in this dealer start-up program. If it were based on that, then it would be a successful program providing opportunities for qualified individuals."

Mr. Carman shook his head, stunned by Christopher's recounting. Then he cracked a little smile, breaking the intensity of the conversation.

"Sounds like the lights are on but nobody's home!" he laughed.

Mr. Carman's guest smiled politely. He was listening with quiet intent, hands folded on his chest, and Christopher could sense tension building. He hesitated to speak further, but Mr. Carman nudged him on. "Please continue, Christopher."

"Ford has provided these dealers with funding and given them the opportunity to succeed as automobile dealers with very little accountability for results," Christopher went on. "Ford seems to be okay with the concept of the DD program, even though it has very poor business results because it is managed irresponsibly. Even with all that Ford provides to many of the DD program dealers, when they have the opportunity to use discretionary Ford products, many of these dealers lack loyalty to Ford and consistently choose to use non-Ford products such as financing, extended warranties, bulk oil, accessories, et cetera.

"The core business model must focus on experience, knowledge of the business, and a track record of success along with a history of demonstrating the ability to get the job done. Often times, when DD dealers were installed, some of our best minority employees were overlooked. We had strong minority candidates inside Ford who should have been given the opportunity to go retail. It's like legal immigration versus illegal immigration, where people go through a certain process of immigration and then emerge as good solid citizens. Within a big corporation, and this isn't just Ford, when you have someone who has not done the right things, has not followed the rules nor earned their stripes, and they jump ahead of someone else who has done those things, solely because of diversity, it is just like amnesty to the illegal immigrant, and it sends the wrong message.

"And that's what we've done with diversity. We've sent the wrong message to our employees. This fosters an environment of inequality and distrust.

"I believe it's risky when a company decides to hire, promote, or put in a place of power an employee or business partner based only on their gender, race, or ethnicity. We should assist diverse candidates, but ultimately performance and skill sets of employees should trump gender, race, ethnicity, or other criteria" concluded Christopher. He sat back in his chair and took a sip of tea.

All of a sudden, Mr. Carman's guest, who had been sitting next to him, listening quietly, pounded his fist on the table, shattering the silence like an earthquake in a glass factory. His powerful voice reverberated throughout the manor.

"They got it all wrong! They have taken what I said and scandalized it! They completely misunderstood what I was trying to tell them! I shared my dream with them, my dream which they quote over and over again — that one day, every valley shall be exalted, every hill and mountain shall be made low, the rough places will be made plain, and the crooked places will be made straight, and the glory of the Lord shall be revealed, and all flesh shall see it together. Not blacks, or whites, or segmented minorities but all people under one God. ALL people! I will not rest until I am certain beyond all doubt that they understand," continued the man with a trembling force. His voice echoed throughout the manor, out the door, into the valley and over the hills. Christopher hoped his voice could also be heard echoing throughout the offices of management at Ford's world headquarters.

The man continued, "I said that in spite of the difficulties and frustrations of the moment, I still have a dream. It is a dream deeply rooted in the American Dream and that one day this nation will rise up and live out the true meaning of its creed — we hold these truths to be self-evident, that all men are created equal. Equality must not be a weapon used to discriminate. Doing so is a crime against humanity and a grave sin in the eyes of God.

"Christopher, you must go back and tell them again what I said, because I will not rest until they get it right, until they understand. Remind them again, and again, that when we let freedom ring, when we let it ring from every village and every hamlet, from every state and every city, we will be able to speed up that day when all of God's children, black men and white men, Jews and Gentiles, Protestants and Catholics, will be able to join hands and sing, 'free at last, free at last! Thank God Almighty, we are free at last!' Remind them over and over until they truly understand."

Christopher lowered his head thinking about how far astray America had gone using the banner of 'diversity.' When he looked back up, the man was gone. Christopher placed his elbows on the table and held his head in his hands. He closed his eyes. *Am I imagining all of this, or was this magnificent man really who my heart tells me he was? What's going on with me? Is the dream inside me so strong that I can will all this to happen? Maybe as Shakespeare said, the world is a stage and we are all actors. And if it isn't a dream, I have been entrusted with a major role and a great responsibility.*

Mr. Carman began to cough spasmodically and held on to the chair railing for strength to stand up. Christopher had seen Mr. Carman's health weaken as the days passed.

"Christopher, Ford's diversity program seems to have started off as a well-intentioned initiative, but it became misguided. They made a tactical error by ignoring the traditional values of their employees, dealers, and customers with this new-fangled strategy on diversity. That is why the program has failed. Remember that you cannot be all things to all people and cater to the minority at the expense of the majority. That's just bad business, everyone should be treated equally," concluded Mr. Carman.

Albert suddenly appeared with Christopher's overcoat over his arm. It was time to go.

"I look forward to our next meeting, same time, same place," Mr. Carman told Christopher, as he waved good-bye.

"Do the right thing at the right time
and expect the right results."
— Mr. Carman

CHAPTER EIGHT

COMPENSATION

*"If money is your hope for independence you will never have it.
The only real security that a man will have in this world
is a reserve of knowledge, experience, and ability."*
— *Henry Ford*

THE WEATHER WAS unusually cold for a spring day. When Christopher arrived back at Fairlane Manor, the winds had picked up, and the fog in front of the house was so dense you could barely see its form, except for the white smoke circling out of the chimney. Today seemed different from all the others. Albert had been waiting to greet him at the front entrance.

"You and Mr. Carman will be dining alone, Mr. Hope. Mr. Carman wasn't up for any visitors. He was quite busy this morning working on the generator. He wanted to lunch only with you today," explained Albert.

"What seems to be the problem with the generator? Can I give him a hand?" he offered.

"Oh no, sir, no need. It will all work out. But thank you kindly," replied Albert.

As the days passed by, Christopher was gaining a sense of confidence around Albert and Mr. Carman. He was comfortable at Fairlane Manor. It felt almost like home to him, different from the modernized Fairlane Manor he had known before meeting Mr. Carman.

He knew his way to the cloakroom, where he hung up his coat right next to Mr. Carman's. He glanced up at the old grandfather clock and noticed that the hour hand was still halted at seven on the nose; he didn't bother to look at his watch. He knew exactly what time it was. And then the clock chimed seven times. He counted each chime, step by step, as he walked with Albert into the dining hall where Mr. Carman was waiting for him.

Christopher had begun to develop a taste and liking for soybeans and found them to have soothing and healing qualities. He sipped his tea slowly, immersed in the moment and more aware of his surroundings than ever before. The fire intensified, casting shadows on the walls. The lights flickered. He thought he had heard music playing, the old kind of melodies that the AM radio had played in his car when Mr. Carman rescued him. It was coming from a room somewhere down the long dark hallway. The humming noise he had once heard before, which sounded like a generator of sort, was louder today. *That's probably the generator Mr. Carman was working on this morning*, he thought. Taking his notepad and pen from his jacket pocket, Christopher placed them on the table. He began to share his grief with Mr. Carman about his colleague and friend, John, who had been given an early retirement package, and then launched into his view of the failures in the compensation system at Ford. Mr. Carman listened compassionately, again troubled by what Christopher was sharing with him and bothered by what seemed to be a cough that just wouldn't quit.

"I believe compensation must be tied to tangible results and performance measures. There must be accountability," stated Christopher. "Rainmakers — those producing results — must be identified and developed. At the same time, calculated risk-taking and accountability must be woven into the environment and must replace the current don't 'rock the boat' strategy. We need results-oriented managers with a true sense of passion for the business. We need managers focused on doing the right things rather than politically correct managers who spend their time try-ing not to offend anyone and more time working on getting their next job than doing their current one. Some managers spend more time trying to look like things are right than doing the right things. There needs to be an overhaul of the compensation system tied to positive business results rather than political correctness."

"In my experience, in the old days," Mr. Carman explained. "Man-agers were servant leaders with a long-term view and allegiance to the people. If they are primarily in it for the money, they will never be success-ful over the long haul."

"You're absolutely right, sir," Christopher jumped in. "At Ford, com-pensation for many of the employees is no longer based on performance or achieving business results, and the promotion system seems to moti-vate the wrong kinds of behavior and causes us to lose many of our top performers.

"Let me explain how Ford's compensation system works. It used to function well, but then things shifted in the early 1980's. Compensation, or what we call the 'pay plan,' was based on achieving specific targets and business results. Managers were graded on how their dealers performed in their zone — not just for their management style. Division managers were paid based on how their division performed. However, some senior management resented this because they thought that the company's re-sults were based on their own great management abilities and that these results had little to do with their employees' performance. Therefore, they developed an idea which they called 'merit planning.' It sounded good and was originally another well-intentioned program. However, it ended up being administered more like an entitlement program as managers handed out similar pay raises to almost everyone, paying little attention to performance. The spread between the top performers' compensation and the lowest performers became less than three percent. The spread was unrealistic for the variance in employee contributions. The company couldn't put their money where the production was — to reward those who were really performing. So everyone got a watered-down 'merit plan.' Employees did not perceive an accurate relationship between their performance and their compensation. Management described this 'merit plan' as a great improvement and told us that we would be more motivated and successful."

"What happened to the middle guys, the ones who actually generate revenue?" Mr. Carman asked.

"The top managers got more than they should have," answered Christopher. "Then, because of our posturing with the UAW and our unwillingness to have them be angry with us as they often were at GM, the UAW was given more than they should have had. The result was the middle managers — those who were actually working with the dealers and achieving results — got crunched. There is only 100 percent of a dollar, and no one at either end was willing to give up their percentage," he explained.

"The promotion system is even more complex and bizarre. Ford, as many large companies used to have, has a system called right-of-assignment. This means that in order to go up to the next grade level, you may have to relocate to another part of the country and often simply at the behest of some misguided manager. Or worse, when an insecure manager viewed you as an up-and-coming leader, they might ship you out for no business reason, but rather to protect their empire so you would not pose a threat. Most of the time, these opportunities were classified as developmental or lateral moves, not promotions, so you were not actually getting a promotion in terms of job responsibilities or pay increase. If you were not willing to relocate, you were not considered loyal or top management material, despite your performance metrics. Each relocation cost the company $50,000 to $250,000 in relocation expenses and incentives. In order to move up in the company, in many instances, you had to move to a new geographic location, even on a lateral basis in title or responsibility.

In addition, to move up in Ford long-term, you also had to serve time in Dearborn.

"As a result, we have had many demoralized employees who had to leave their community where they were performing at a high level to start all over in another part of the country. This placed tremendous stress on the home life, particularly since today there are more and more two career couples. The company would rationalize that it valued the employee's family and personal life and then at the same time expect the employee to uproot their family every few years. We lost some of our best future leaders who were unwilling to stay with the company with this archaic approach of moving around to move up.

"It seemed that many of the relocations were just to have some experience pass through and get a box checked on your employee profile. In quite a number of cases, when the person was relocated, they did not have the right skill-sets for the job and they were unable to perform, leaving the other employees in that location to fill in for the new person who could not do it. This caused tensions among those doing the new person's job for them, and made them more resentful of the new person joining that location. This was a 'lose-lose' situation.

"The other side of the coin was that because so many employees did not want to move from the location they loved, they would not perform at top levels because they feared if they did too good of a job they would be promoted and have to relocate their family. So Ford lost great people who left the company to keep from having to move and lost performance from others who did not want to leave Ford but did not want to have to move if they excelled and were targeted to relocate. If you added the disincentive of relocation for excellence to the small difference in compensation between an average performance and an outstanding one — roughly three percent of your compensation, why would anyone want to contribute their best? This created a lowest common denominator mind-set when we should have been creating leaders at all levels and in all locations, since few, if any, companies have too many leaders," said Christopher.

"Another problem with the incentives and lack of accountability is in our marketing relationships. We have had hot shot marketing leaders in the company come in, only planning to stay for a short time. No one was watching the store and holding them accountable. They overpaid vendors for marketing services in order to build a relationship with them; strangely enough, they ended up working there when they left Ford. As soon as they are held accountable or asked to produce, they bolt like gold miners going to a new mine.

"So this right-of-assignment rule and your overall promotion system seems crazy, especially in order to attract the good young people of today. It also seems that it would have a negative impact on the employees developing long-term relationships with the dealers in their markets. The company should value employees that produce great results, while fostering relationships with the dealers and their communities," said Mr. Carman.

"For some strange reason, the company seems to fear the dealer relationship — like they can't get too close," Christopher explained.

"That's complete nonsense!" quipped Mr. Carman. "How can you have good dealer partners without a relationship built on trust, integrity, and consistency?"

"You're so wise, Mr. Carman. We should be encouraging and rewarding our employees who thrive with their dealer partners. Without successful dealers, how do we sell and service our cars and trucks? That should be more important than if someone happens to be willing to relocate." Christopher suggested.

"It seems that the company's management has confused activity with accomplishment. I always said that a rocking chair has activity, but it's not going anywhere," said Mr. Carman.

"Exactly! And just think of the great employees we could have retained and the millions of dollars wasted on unnecessary relocation expenses!" explained Christopher.

"There are no two ways about it. Compensation and promotion must be tied to performance," injected Mr. Carman. "That's the bottom line."

"An effective, but short-lived, example of tying rewards to performance was a program the company launched called the 'Continuous Improvement Recognition Program.' It saved Ford a ton of money," Christopher continued.

"And what was that?" asked Mr. Carman.

"Any employee could present an idea to improve efficiency or save costs. It got every employee engaged in trying to cut costs and improve bottom line results. Many great ideas and actions were submitted. The program cost Ford about a million dollars a year in compensation to those who submitted ideas, but it saved Ford hundreds of millions of dollars as they implemented the new ideas. But senior management ended up cutting the program because they thought the company was paying too much money to the mid-manager and non-manager levels, and top managers couldn't participate," Christopher explained.

Mr. Carman shook his head.

"What? Are you telling me that the company cut a program which cost only one million a year but saved them hundreds of millions of dollars? Can't they count? On top of that, it empowered employees and engaged them more fully in the business. Are they crazy? Have they forgotten the purpose of it all?" exclaimed Mr. Carman, his voice cracking. He removed his handkerchief from his vest pocket and held it up to his mouth. He began to cough, having a hard time catching his breath.

Christopher paused and waited for Mr. Carman to regain his composure. Albert suddenly entered the dining hall with a handful of logs, placing them on the fire where the flames had begun to dwindle.

"We'll get this fire going, sir, and it will be much warmer in here in a few minutes."

"Thanks, Albert," replied Mr. Carman, as his cough began to subside. The new firewood began to catch on and crackle and as the room warmed up nicely, they resumed their conversation.

"Unfortunately, many Ford leaders have become self-serving, short-term thinkers with a keen and constant eye only for lining their own pockets. There has been a shift away from pay for performance to pay for potential ability to perform and pay for diversity, with little accountability for results," Christopher continued.

Mr. Carman was exasperated. "This compensation and promotion model will wear you down. They are tossing their employees overboard!" he exclaimed. "Now, what about the dealers — how do they fare with all of Ford's decisions?"

"Our dealers are having to restructure so they can still be profitable with a reduction in market share. And keep in mind that a percentage or point in market share in the auto industry is generally considered to be worth $2.8 billion in revenue over a one-year period. Even in down years, a point improvement means more than 100,000 added vehicle sales.

"Many will be forced to take on another franchise to offset the lost revenue, and others will go out of business. Without profitable dealers, we will never reach our sales goals. Yes, Ford allows them to have their franchise, but historically we have made tons of money off their hard work, and we would not exist as a company today without them. Look at the other major manufacturers — do any of them exist without distributors or dealers? This current situation is really very tough on our dealers. Their existing facilities were constructed based on a 20-plus percent market share. They are very anxious because they realize the dealer ranks need to be reduced to increase efficiency and promote mutual profitability. Unfortunately, some of our long standing and loyal Ford dealers are going to be out of business," explained Christopher

"Ford needs to provide incentives to all levels of the company for progress towards goals and objectives, and not just for profits," Mr. Carman explained. "Ford needs to reward top performers and leaders with not only a fair share of the compensation pie, but also with recognition for all they do. If you do this, perhaps you can stop the exodus of talented people leaving because they perceive they are not valued. The company must also spend time and energy trying to communicate more effectively with their employees and dealers as you work through this challenging time period," said Mr. Carman.

"We desperately need a strategic plan that our employees and dealers believe in and will rally around. Keep a good record of these notes, Christopher, and everything you are sharing with me. They will be very useful and important in the coming days ahead," he said. "Right now, I've got some work to do on the generator today, and not a lot of time to fix it."

"Sure I couldn't take a look at it with you? I'm really pretty handy with motors and electricity. I'm sort of a hands-on kind of guy," smiled Christopher.

Mr. Carman laughed.

"Thanks again, son. That's mighty thoughtful of you, but I think that Ford needs some fixing too, so you go head back to headquarters — they really need you there. And don't worry about me — I'll be on my way real soon."

A cold draft blew through the dining hall, and the lights flickered.

It was time to go. They walked side by side to the entrance. Christopher fetched his coat from the cloakroom.

"I'll see you tomorrow then, same time, same place," Mr. Carman said to Christopher, as he waved goodbye to him from the front porch.

> *"Rewards and recognition should be earned*
> *by getting the desired results." — Mr. Carman*

CHAPTER SEVEN

THE UNION

*"You will find men who want to be carried on
the shoulders of others, who think that the world
owes them a living. They don't seem to see that we must all
lift together and pull together." — Henry Ford*

CHRISTOPHER PLANNED TO talk with Mr. Carman about the union at their lunch appointment later that day. As he was preparing for their meeting, he thought about the thousands of dedicated and proud Ford and UAW workers he had come to know over the years. He remembered the diehard loyalty and the spirit that most of them possessed. In fact, he truly believed that if most of them were cut, they would bleed Ford blue. He wondered what would become of all the friends that he had made in the factories, plants, and parts depots. He thought that there was a special relationship between Ford and the UAW membership due in large part because of how well the Ford family had treated them over the years.

On several of his many assignments while moving up through Ford, he had the privilege of having his office located on site at the plants and depots alongside UAW workers. The vast majority of the employees were good, loyal, and proud people who had unknowingly been working under a bad contract. Christopher knew that if these contracts were not altered, they could surely kill the golden goose of the Ford Motor Company. Many jobs and livelihoods were at stake.

Many of his union friends would, from time to time, share with him that they knew the union deal was bad for Ford in that it favored the union too much. But his friends also knew that pointing out any union-friendly flaws in a union meeting would be suicidal. As a result, most union employees had chosen to ride this bus for as long as they could.

Christopher had heard many stories from his friends about the crazy things that some of their UAW co-workers would do. Most of the stories were innocuous incidents such as an employee simply not coming to work after a night at a ball game or after a party weekend. Some of the stories centered on employees who just tended to hang out during the work day without focus and without doing their job. Inevitably, these stories were concluded by his friends saying something like, "and you know what frustrates the Ford managers the most is that they can't enforce good work behaviors because of the current UAW contract which protects even those who don't work!"

Working for Ford seemed like a game to a small percentage of dissident employees who felt as if they had a license to do whatever they could to frustrate management without any repercussions. Some constantly called for the hard-line tactics of the past in an attempt to rejuvenate the labor movement and take a stand against shifting economic conditions.

Christopher knew that there was a time when unions were needed to protect the rights and safety of employees. In recent years, however, the focus had shifted from protection to holding companies hostage for higher pay for less work, more benefits, and less accountability — all at a cost of declining competitiveness of their employer compared to foreign manufacturers. It was high time for the UAW to carve out a new purpose for itself, one that if properly executed, could serve as the foundation for a brighter future.

As he was sifting and sorting though his thoughts, the telephone rang, reminding him that he had a busy day ahead of him.

"Christopher here," he answered.

"Good morning, Mr. Hope. It's Albert. I'm calling to ask you if it wouldn't be an imposition to come to the manor for tea this afternoon, rather than lunch. Mr. Carman has invited a special guest, and unfortunately she will not be able to make it in time for lunch."

"I think anytime this afternoon would be fine," he replied, as he quickly clicked open his calendar on his laptop. "This afternoon would be great. I can move my schedule up and work straight through lunch. That will free me up to leave earlier today. What time would be convenient for Mr. Carman and his guest?"

"Shall we say four o'clock then?" confirmed Albert.

"Sure thing!" Christopher replied.

"Mr. Carman will be expecting you," said Albert.

She? thought Christopher. *Who could she be?* he wondered with a playful curiosity, because he only remembered seeing men around the manor on most of his visits.

The afternoon flew by. He glanced at his watch. Four o'clock was rapidly approaching. The sun was lowering in the sky. It was time to leave for his meeting at Fairlane Manor. He took his coat off the hook and walked toward the elevators. As he drove out of the parking garage into the busy Dearborn traffic, he noticed a street vendor at the corner selling flowers. Christopher stopped and bought a small bouquet of red roses for Mr. Carman's guest.

The weather began to change once again, as it had all the days before on his way to the manor. In no time, he arrived at the front gates where an attendant came out to park his car. Albert arrived at the top of the stairs to greet him and take his coat. Once inside, he walked down the hallway to the dining room as the grandfather clock chimed its melancholy notes.

The table was set for three, with fine china and trays of scones, cookies, tea sandwiches, jams, and a large pot of soybean tea. Seated at the table were Mr. Carman and a sophisticated, stately woman with a fur shawl wrapped around her shoulders. A strand of large white pearls adorned her elegant black dress. Her wide brimmed, oval felt hat was tipped to the side of her head and decorated with an elaborately bejeweled pin. The lady had a very striking face with penetrating dark and kind eyes and a great big smile. An aura of light radiated from her presence.

Christopher offered the lady the bouquet of red roses.

"Oh, how thoughtful! My husband and I have nurtured a rose garden for many years at our estate in Hyde Park. I've kept a close watch on them, you know, as they require constant care," said the lady, placing the rose bouquet on her lap.

Christopher sat down, then glanced up again to catch another quick look at the lady seated at his side. There was no question in his mind as to who she was. And who could he tell? Who would believe him? Was it important anyway? *If it was a dream, vision, reality, or his perception of reality, did it really matter?* he reflected. Christopher's job was to be the ultimate spin doctor, living in a world where reality was about perception, dictated by those who had the power and the money. With each meeting with Mr. Carman, Christopher's journey for the truth took on more significance and meaning than he could have ever anticipated. This was about more than writing press stories and the opportunity to vent years of frustrations. His search had led him on a gut-wrenching and challenging path.

"Well, as we had planned, I'd like to share with you the state of things at Ford today, regarding our relationship with the United Auto Workers," said Christopher, his voice somewhat hesitant as a shyness came over him.

Somehow instinctively, Mr. Carman always knew how to break the ice and make everyone feel relaxed. "You know what Will Rogers once said?" he said with a silly grin: "Live in such a way that you would not be ashamed to sell your parrot to the town gossip."

Everyone laughed, and then the lady turned to Christopher and said, "So tell me, Mr. Hope, about the state of affairs of the company and our nation today in relation to the union and human rights. Although I have many years of experience in this regard, the world has changed quite a bit, and I would like to learn more about where we have evolved," she said.

"Madam, it's my honor, and I hope I will not be offensive in my attempt to be honest and frank," explained Christopher. "There are many challenges facing Ford regarding the union and human rights. The economic deals we've cut with the union are financial suicide. The union is no longer designed to help the little guy.

"Our present contract and relationship with the UAW is a set-up for failure," he continued. "The current arrangements with the unions in the U.S. have driven jobs out of the country, and it keeps us from being competitive in a super competitive industry."

Christopher's mouth was parched. He paused to sip of his tea and continued.

"If labor costs as a percentage of sales are growing faster than your profit margin, you know you are heading down the wrong path. It's simply not sustainable in the long run. The U.S. auto industry pays among the highest manufacturing wages in the world. Japanese car companies, operating in the U.S., designed factories roughly half the size of American assembly plants, with half the employees and cost, yet produced the same number of vehicles. The union would not allow the American automotive companies to do that. The UAW continued to demand that the American automakers pay workers displaced by new technology or other changes in production strategy. This led to the creation of the infamous Jobs Bank program. This essentially handcuffed the Detroit Three from closing plants and actually encouraged efforts to sustain high levels of production even when demand dropped. The idea was that if the UAW workers believed they couldn't be fired if the company became more efficient, then they might embrace the new production methods. We all know that didn't work, and the Jobs Bank became little more than a welfare-type system for workers who had nothing more to contribute because market share declines made them expendable."

"It's no wonder so many jobs are going overseas," Mr. Carman interjected.

"Being new to this country and non-union gave the foreign automakers tremendous cost advantages in a capital and technology intensive business like auto manufacturing," Christopher continued. "With major subsidies from host states, Honda, Toyota, Nissan, BMW, Mercedes and Hyundai built brand new assembly plants in our country that were designed to use the latest manufacturing processes and technology. The real advantage for these companies was that their new non-union employees were paid less per hour than UAW employees. This was a major cost advantage for the transplants not only because they paid them less per hour, but because non-union companies didn't have to bear the additional costs for health care and pensions for thousands of retirees. Imagine spending billions of dollars each year to fund your pension and health care obligations while competition shows up in America with none of these restrictions and lucrative subsidies from host states. Deep down, the Detroit Three still believed the Japanese could be stopped by import quotas just as

Japan stopped us in their country. They never believed the Japanese could replicate their low-cost manufacturing systems in America. They knew that the lower pricing of Japanese cars was largely the result of automation, non-union employees, and unfair trading practices. They figured the Japanese would have just a little niche of small cars and the market share would be contained as customers grew out of their small car phase of life."

Mr. Carman turned to Christopher, his piercing blue eyes looking directly into his.

"For Pete's sake! It's time to be fair!" exclaimed Mr. Carman. "You cannot continue to subsidize overinflated UAW wages and benefits at the expense of being competitive in the marketplace. There should be equality for all workers with a fair distribution of compensation, accountability, and sacrifice!"

"Management and labor seem to operate independently rather than in concert," said Christopher. "Shouldn't we all be operating under the same umbrella and with the same benefits?"

"You raise a great question, Mr. Hope. Perhaps I can shed some light on the matter," the lady offered. "You know, when my husband was alive, I traveled extensively around the nation, visiting relief projects, surveying working and living conditions, and then reporting my observations to the President. I was fortunate to exercise my own political and social influence. I became an advocate of the rights and needs of the poor, of minorities, and of the disadvantaged. I participated in the League of Women Voters and joined the Women's Trade Union League. I have always championed humanitarian causes.

"Besides wearing many hats as an author, political activist, columnist, teacher, diplomat, and First Lady, I was also a worker and a union member. What you are telling me is very disturbing indeed. I spent my entire life as a champion of workers around the world. I was eternally grateful for the generous support of the men and women of the labor movement. They valued my support and friendship. They worked with me in completing the Universal Declaration of Human Rights as delegates to the United Nations in 1948. From my first meeting with the Women's Trade Union League in 1919 until 1962, I always quoted the AFL-CIO slogan — 'One of us.'"

Christopher took notes, writing at a furious pace, wanting to record every word the lady said.

"I've had close and positive working relationships with union leaders, union members — especially union women — and with those seeking social justice and human rights in the workplace at home and abroad," stated the woman. "Working in partnership, we overcame barriers of class, race, and gender. I truly believed that what I did on a national and international level, everyone could and should do on a local level. Where, after all, do universal human rights begin but in small places, close to home, in the everyday world of human beings, the neighborhoods they live in, the schools or colleges they attend, the factories, farms, or offices where they work, where every man, woman, and child seeks to have equal justice and opportunity, equal dignity without discrimination? Unless these rights have meaning there, they have little meaning anywhere. Without concerted citizen action to uphold them close to home, we shall look in vain for progress in the larger world. I understood the world I lived in, because it belonged to me. The world you live in belongs to you and your contemporaries. I cannot judge your actions based on circumstances of another time."

The lady's soft and nostalgic mood was fading. She tightened her lips and straightened her posture.

Mr. Carman began to cough; once again his breathing had become difficult. Albert appeared and served Mr. Carman another hot cup of soybean tea. As Mr. Carman settled down, the lady continued.

"In my days, the labor conditions for workers were something that people in your time would consider criminal and third world. My advocacy for the union and for human rights covered basic human dignity and survival. It was hard-lined because of the greed of the employers and the lack of basic human needs for food, shelter, warmth, safety, security, and fair compensation. In your world, the union has taken the wrong direction, moving away from its responsible purpose to protect the basic rights of the common man, and has become a political tool for greed, empowerment, and manipulation. I would have never supported such an atrocity of justice. This is not the America that my husband and I loved and served with complete trust and conviction. The union exists to protect and defend the weak, not to hold the company hostage for more money for union officials. Wake up, my beloved America, before it's too late!"

A shroud of embarrassment and remorse fell over Christopher. He felt a sense of collective responsibility and he searched his mind for answers and solutions.

"The creation and approval of a realistic Ford contract that will allow flexibility to each in an ever-changing market without overburdening either party is the responsibility of both Ford and the UAW management. The UAW management in conjunction with Ford has endangered the entire future of Ford Motor Company with the last deal they agreed to," Christopher explained.

"The solutions seem simple to me," observed Mr. Carman. "Employees should work side-by-side and learn to respect each other more. Ford's production line workers should be allowed greater latitude to perform different tasks. Ford should encourage and reward workers to find more cost-effective and better ways to assemble cars and trucks. Ford should continue to improve safety in our plants and make jobs less tedious. The company needs to chase out costs that rivals don't have to pay!"

"Each side has a big stake in cooperating with the other right now," added the lady.

"If the boat sinks, we all go down together," quipped Mr. Carman.

"You're both absolutely right. Either side has the potential to destroy Ford," Christopher said.

Mr. Carman looked directly at the lady seated beside him and said:

"Your acceptance of my invitation to Fairlane Manor means a great deal to me. I am grateful and delighted you came. There is also a personal reason that I asked you to come here today. Many years ago I opposed issues that you and your late husband advocated, such as the New Deal, and as you very well know, I have had my own strong disagreements with the UAW and other issues during my lifetime. I too had a dream to run for the highest office in the land and to lead our great nation, but I quickly discovered that a political career is like breakfast at the Coliseum. No one escapes the cruelty of the beast. I've always said that history was bunk. Why? Because historians write the supposed facts many years after the heroes or villains are gone. Historians, in my opinion, are basically fictional writers, slanting, filtering, and spinning the so-called facts. Values and principles are eternal and can never be compromised. They stand the test of time."

Christopher nodded in agreement. Mr. Carman continued. "And I have faced my destiny for the choices I've made during my lifetime. Those who are entrusted with the responsibility to lead others will be held accountable for their decisions and judged accordingly. If I have been offensive to you and others during my lifetime, or caused harm to any one in any way, I ask forgiveness for being such a fool. Because in the final moment, when the mortal clock is silenced, on whatever side of the picket line we stand here on earth, we will be held accountable for our thoughts, words, and actions, to the ultimate CEO of all creation. Madam, you are an outstanding example to workers everywhere of selfless leadership devoted to the well-being of others. Please give my very best regards to the President."

The fire burned even brighter now, cracking and spewing embers onto the floor. The lady reached out her hand to Mr. Carman and placed it on his, in a gentle embrace. They looked into each other's eyes and smiled. Then the lady lowered her head to smell the roses.

It was time to go.

Christopher said good-bye to the lady who was escorted off by Albert into a Model A that had been waiting for her at the front entrance. He took his coat from the cloakroom and headed toward his car, which was also waiting for him outside the gates.

"I'll see you tomorrow then," Mr. Carman told Christopher, waving good-bye from the front porch.

"Beware the C.A.V.E. people — people who are Collectively Against Virtually Everything." — Mr. Carman

Mexico
$FORD
Chin
Taiwa
Japa
Austral
dle East
Other countries
USA
Globalization

CHAPTER SIX

GLOBALIZATION

*"A business absolutely devoted to service will have
only one worry about profits.
They will be embarrassingly large."*
— *Henry Ford*

THE WEEK QUICKLY passed by. Christopher had made a list of the topics he hoped to cover before Mr. Carman departed for his journey. He wondered if Mr. Carman would invite another friend over for lunch today and, if so, who the mystery guest would be.

As usual, Mr. Carman was waiting for him on the porch, sitting in the rocking chair. Next to him, in the other chair, was a man of worldly distinction. Both men were engrossed in an animated conversation.

Mr. Carman and his friend waved to him as he walked up the stairs toward the porch.

"I'd like you to meet one of my closest friends. He grew up near Dearborn, on around ninety acres of some of the best farmland in these parts," explained Mr. Carman proudly. His friend smiled warmly at Christopher and stood to help his buddy from the rocking chair.

The man was tall and handsome, with a perfectly manicured mustache and broad, chiseled features. His brown hair was neatly combed to the side. He wore an impeccable brown three-piece vested suit of the same old-fashioned style Christopher had become accustomed to seeing in the company of Mr. Carman. He spoke with a cultured accent and in a reassuring tone.

"Come on, old friend, let's get out of this damp weather and go inside by the warm fire," suggested the man as he walked arm-in-arm with Mr. Carman into the dining hall. Albert took everyone's coats and hats. The towering old grandfather clock chimed seven times, but Christopher didn't bother to check his watch today.

As Albert served lunch, Christopher was ready with his notepad and pen. The conversation immediately led to the topic of globalization. He was again amazed at Mr. Carman's uncanny knowledge and hoped to discuss Ford's recent tunnel vision on the subject of globalization. As expected, Mr. Carman had clear thoughts on the subject and had brought a friend who could add much needed insight.

"My buddy here," said Mr. Carman, "was the founder of one of the first global corporations in America and was an important contributor to North American economic growth in the 20th century. You could say that his products have covered countless miles and have quite a track record. We were members, along with another friend of ours whom you met a few days ago, of a club that made us privy to exclusive business opportunities. We could call each other from any location and ask permission to purchase a building or other items on our word alone. We didn't even need a handshake."

"Ah! Such relationships rarely exist in the business world today," said Mr. Carman's friend, with a look of nostalgia coming over him. Mr. Carman motioned to Christopher, inviting him to get the conversation rolling.

"So tell me," Mr. Carman said. "Since we have my dear friend here who was once on the cutting edge of globalization for our country, how is Ford handling its global opportunities today?"

"Well," said Christopher, not sure where to begin. "I guess you could sum up Ford's take on globalization by saying that Ford has forgotten to keep the main thing, the main thing!"

"Well, what do you mean by that?" Mr. Carman asked, sounding intrigued.

"Yes, do tell," his friend prompted.

"The days of operating regionally need to come to an end," Christopher exclaimed. "We currently have American vehicles for the U.S. market, European vehicles for Europe, Asian vehicles for Asia, and so on. It's time to leverage our global assets, innovation, technology and scale to deliver world class products for every market."

"Right on, please continue," urged Mr. Carman.

"There is way too much inefficiency and waste in our current vehicle development and manufacturing operations," Christopher added. "We must deconstruct the old, staggeringly expensive operating model where we developed a full range of unique products for each market around the world. In order to thrive in the future, we must have more high-volume global platforms. That simply means more vehicles built on the same underpinnings. Global platforms are a much more affordable way to produce a larger variety of vehicles using the same core components," he concluded.

"You remember what a great American writer once said," barked Mr. Carman. "Shoot for the moon and even if you miss it you will land among the stars."

The three men all chuckled.

Christopher continued with his thought. "By leveraging economies of scale across the globe, we could bring a full product lineup to market while significantly holding down development, engineering, purchasing and production costs. It also means Ford could negotiate much better prices from suppliers because we would be ordering far more components. It would even reduce tooling costs. The scale benefits would be tremendous for everyone involved," he added.

"Now we're making sense. Just imagine the positive effects on serviceability and product quality," added Mr. Carman's good friend.

"As we ramp up for this global transformation, we must look at every potential market for opportunities to sell from our current worldwide production. Initially, we should establish a tight organization in a new market with minimal sales and service support to export products until the market can be established to support a full-service sales operation," Christopher explained.

"We need to do a better job of evaluating potential export markets and establish a system to project the return on investment. If cash is tight and we can't project profitable business from a venture, we need to set aside our ego and make the good business decision to opt out of that market. We need to resist the temptation to go to an alleged future 'hot spot' market just because the competition is there or is planning on going there."

"Now, you're rolling" said Mr. Carman's friend.

"We should consider partnering with low-cost producers to develop products locally in very small countries using their capital and our name, leveraging their low-cost production advantage with our Ford name and marketing expertise. Ford has a huge edge on brand perception in these newer markets and our favorability rating is very high around our products. People aspire to own a Ford; the brand has a very high level of pricing power and reputation.

"We also need to consider the 'import model' used to create production facilities in the United States for foreign automotive companies. The strategy is always the same: they request grants, no-interest loans, and subsidies from federal, state, and local governmental agencies. Sometimes they even get the land at no cost. So their start-up costs are 25 to 30 percent cheaper than U.S. based companies. Using the same approach abroad for Ford would help us be much more competitive. Some of these potential foreign partners for Ford would even be willing to offer health care subsidies to bring employment to their area. Global production and marketing may offer opportunities to grow Ford, but it should only be pursued if it is going to be profitable for everyone involved," Christopher said.

"Another issue is whether we have free trade or fair trade." asked Christopher, clearly showing frustration in his voice about the many closed markets around the globe. "While we hear about free trade, it certainly isn't fair trade. Japan and Korea seem proud of their 'barriers to entry,' tariffs, quotas and limited openness to outside vehicle producers. The 'barriers to entry' are obstacles that are even more effective than the tariffs and quotas, and include major inspections, complicated distribution systems and taxation. While on the surface Japan and Korea say they no longer restrict U.S. imports, they sure do a great job creating barriers. In Korea, a practice that appears to target importers still exists today — Korean citizens who purchase an import vehicle have their tax returns audited. For all intents and purposes, the Japanese and Korean markets are closed to everyone from the outside. No one gets a foothold," Christopher continued. "Here's an example that drives home my point: Ford sells about 2500 vehicles in Korea each year, compared to 330,000 Hyundai/Kia vehicles imported to the U.S. Our automotive trade with Japan is even more lopsided," Christopher concluded.

Mr. Carman jumped in and said, "it seems like the right thing to do is institute a 'golden rule' trade policy — give other countries the same treatment they give us. Washington should have gotten involved."

"Yes, absolutely," agreed Christopher. "Globalization, while a great strategy for business growth, cannot exceed good business judgment in the rate of growth. Standardization of platforms is good and allows a consistent growth strategy to globalize. Research must be executed thoroughly before making decisions as to where to go next with your product.

Evaluations should be made based on return on investment and cost to establish a profitable venture — not just the annual profit and loss. More time needs to be spent analyzing new or emerging markets as well as major competitors.

"Ford has partnered with many companies as part of its globalization strategy, but profits and a reasonable return on investments haven't followed. Most of our partnering ventures, such as the ones with Aston Martin, Jaguar, Land Rover, Mazda and Volvo, soaked up cash like water on an empty sponge. Of course there were some real benefits, but the cash drain far outweighed them. Setting up foreign partnerships was part of our keeping-up-with-the-Joneses syndrome."

Mr. Carman grew pale. He shook his head from side to side in disbelief. "This is completely unacceptable!" exclaimed Mr. Carman. "We need to dance with the one we brought to the party! The blue oval is the only one we need."

Christopher paused until Mr. Carman urged him to continue.

"European engineers from Ford have spent decades perfecting small vehicles that sip gas and are far more refined than the typical American economy box," Christopher continued. "Why not import some of these great cars from Europe to North America? Ford really needs to operate as a boundary-less global company that melds the strengths of all of its far-flung operations."

"I have a question for you, Christopher," interjected Mr. Carman's friend. "We use these terms 'global' and 'globalization' in so many different contexts. How would you define 'globalization' from today's point of view?" asked the man.

"That's a challenging question, sir," Christopher answered. "'Globalization' is a term used to refer to the expansion of economies beyond national borders — in particular, the expansion of production by a firm to many countries around the world. 'Globalization' also refers to the process of manufacturing and/or marketing products around the world, such as in the 'globalization of production,' or the 'global assembly line.' The concept of globalization has given transnational corporations power to reach beyond nation states. Some critics today say that it has the potential to weaken any nation's ability to control corporate practices and flows of capital, set regulations, control balances of trade and exchange rates, or manage domestic economic policy. One of the concerns of the UAW is that globalization has weakened the ability of workers to fight for better wages from fear that employers may relocate to other countries where the cost of labor is less."

"So, you are saying that like many concepts, globalization today has the power to make companies more successful, but also brings with it many complications that must be considered," said Mr. Carman.

"That's a fair assessment indeed," agreed Christopher.

"In my opinion, globalization presents many challenges, but I believe there is a very important overall benefit that comes with it," Mr. Carman's friend added. "Globalization of products leads to global cultures, where various traditions and backgrounds merge and blend, bringing different views, new ideas, and strengths together. America in itself is a model example of the benefit of the globalization of cultures. Our country has thrived by being a melting pot of various cultures. In fact, it could be said that therein lies our greatness. We have inherited this great nation from the sacrifices of hard-working people from all walks of life and cultures. It was they who built our railroads and highways and gave their lives for our freedom. The American Dream was born out of the great benefits of the globalization of cultures. The American Dream is the belief that through hard work and determination, any American can achieve a better life, usually in terms of financial prosperity and enhanced personal freedom. This Dream has always been a major factor in attracting immigrants to the U.S.. According to historians, the rapid economic and industrial expansion of the U.S. is not simply a function of being a resource rich, hard-working, and inventive country, but it's the prospect that any citizen can get a share of the country's wealth if he or she is willing to work hard. So, you see, it is my belief that globalization can be a very good thing."

Mr. Carman nodded in agreement as his friend turned to Christopher.

"I've had an incredible life filled with valuable lessons I learned along the way. I'd like to share a very important principle of mine with you, and please remember to share this with others. The growth and development of people is the highest calling of leadership. Whether we are doing business domestically or aiming to become a global giant, remember that it is only as we develop others that we permanently succeed."

His simple and candid words penetrated to Christopher's heart and into the heart of the problems facing Ford and the American Dream.

It really didn't seem to matter anymore to him if this mystery guest was really the famous inventor he thought he was. There was a far greater purpose for this incredible journey he was on, and he was determined to follow its path to the very end.

Mr. Carman asked to be excused, to end the lunch earlier today. It was time to go.

Christopher's eyes followed the shadowy figure of Mr. Carman's friend as he slowly vanished down the long hallway toward the manor's entrance.

"I'll see you tomorrow then, same time, same place," Mr. Carman reminded Christopher.

Albert walked with Mr. Carman to a room down the hallway, and Christopher let himself out of the manor. Looking through the thick beveled-glass widows out over the porch, he could see flashes of lightning and a thunderstorm approaching. He had almost forgotten to fetch his coat. As usual, his car was ready for him, perfectly parked in the front of the manor, keys in the ignition and with a full tank of gas.

All the way home, he reflected on his conversation on globalization with Mr. Carman and his friend. *What we really need*, he thought, *is a centralized source that evaluates all of our products and opportunities on a global basis. We need* to look at the demands of our markets individually and the cost of marketing all our products and make decisions as to which products go where. Products must be streamlined to a universal specification and built to the level that allows flexibility in marketing. He paused and thought, *though the savings are unlikely to be on the same scale as on the product side, merging the company's global marketing activity would reveal positive results too. Just imagine the benefits of sharing common themes rather than creating things independently in every market around the world like we do now.* He would remember to include these thoughts into his notes from today's conversation as soon as he got back to his office.

"Sometimes our tests become our testimonies, our messes become our messages, and our obstacles become our opportunities."
— Mr. Carman

CHAPTER FIVE

RECAPTURING THE VISION

"Whether you think you can, or that you can't,
you are usually right."
— Henry Ford

THE FOG HUNG heavy over the road, and it looked like rain. As Christopher approached Fairlane Manor, he noticed two vehicles parked outside the gates. One was an official looking, unidentified black limousine with dark tinted windows. An American flag flew on the side of the car, and the license plate on the back read "U.S. Government — Official Business."

The other vehicle wasn't a car at all. It was an American World War II high-ranking army tank. Mr. Carman was not sitting on the front porch today as he usually was. Albert arrived at the entrance to greet him.

"I suggest you hurry on in, Mr. Hope. Mr. Carman's guest today is here on official business and is on a very tight schedule. Your meeting today will be brief and held in the library down the hallway. I will be serving a light lunch in there," instructed Albert.

He took Christopher's coat, then beckoned him to follow as they hurried down the dark hallway. They arrived in front of two soaring mahogany doors. Albert knocked three times. Mr. Carman opened the door, motioning for Christopher to enter. The library walls were stacked with books up to the ceiling that soared at least twenty feet. The room was filled with many antiques and objects from different parts of the world.

On a long table in the center of the room were piled books, maps, diagrams, and all sorts of papers. On an antique side table, Albert had placed a tray with soybean tea and sandwiches.

Standing at the end of the table was a wall of a man wearing an officer's uniform. The first thing Christopher's eyes fixed on were the numerous medals and decorations on his jacket, four stars and one he immediately recognized as a Purple Heart. Christopher's eyes moved up to the pipe dangling from the man's mouth. Then, before he could think or breathe or say anything, the imposingly handsome stranger walked towards him, reaching out his hand, nearly crushing Christopher's in his grip. Christopher felt an electrical energy charge right through him.

"I'd like you to meet my friend, the General," said Mr. Carman.

"Come on in, young man," said the General. "Roll up your sleeves. We've got work to do. The company is in urgent need of a strategic restructuring plan."

Mr. Carman looked at Christopher, and a boyish grin flashed color across his pale face. "You know what Will Rogers used to say: 'Take the diplomacy out of war and the thing would fall flat in a week.'" Laughter broke out but only for a brief moment before seriousness of the meeting set in.

Spread across the long oval table was a detailed chart with graphs and writing on it. An easel and a pointer had been placed next to the table. The General had a long scrolled document under his arm, which he unrolled and clipped on the easel.

"Young man, I suggest you get out your notepad and pen and start writing your notes," he ordered. "Time is of the essence, and in order to save Ford Motor Company and the American Dream, a restructuring plan must be devised and executed very fast.

"There are obviously many issues to address. But at the core of the matter, in our analysis, Ford's leadership seems to function as an empire with the notion of divine powers over the people it is entrusted to serve. To reverse these downward trends, and prevent the impending collapse of this once-upon-a-time great American icon, we must march forward to democratize Ford and implement a strategic plan that will re-establish responsible leadership. This plan should serve as a model plan for every single corporation in America and around the world," outlined the General.

"Let me share some of my leadership experiences during our last world war, and perhaps we can glean some lessons on how to turn things around. Immediately after the Japanese announced their decision to surrender, I was appointed the supreme commander for the Allied Powers to oversee the occupation of Japan. Although technically I was under the authority of an Allied Powers commission, I took my orders from Washington. Rather than establish an American military government to rule Japan during the occupation, I decided to employ the existing Japanese government. I issued several direct orders to Japanese government officials but allowed them to manage the country as long as they followed the occupation goals developed in Potsdam and Washington. I realized that imposing a new order on the island nation would be a difficult task, even with Japanese cooperation. It would be impossible for foreigners to dictate radical changes to 80 million resentful people.

"But we could not simply encourage the growth of democracy. We had to make sure that it grew. Under the old constitution, government flowed downward from the emperor, who held the supreme authority, to those to whom he had delegated power. It was a dictatorship to begin with, and a hereditary one, and the people existed to serve it. Sound familiar?" asked the General, looking directly at Christopher.

"Yes, sir, it sure does," Christopher answered.

"Remember that 'absolute power corrupts absolutely' and that the basic keys to success are always the same," explained the General. "If Ford and others, who had surrendered to the enemy of greed and pride, follow the steps outlined in this strategic restructuring plan, they can be liberated once again, back on the road to freedom and success, simply because they have chosen to do the right things."

The General pointed to the chart on the board and read each item out loud. Mr. Carman stood proudly by the General's side while Christopher took down the notes.

THE FORD ONE TEAM
RESTRUCTURING PLAN
Ford Motor Company, Corporate America, and Global Partners

Leadership/Culture

- Provide consistent and stable leadership while developing leaders at all levels.
- Ensure all leaders/managers are servant-leaders.
- Treat everyone equally and fairly based on democratic principles.
- Tie compensation to productivity and contribution at all levels — consistently balanced.
- Hire and promote based on a person's ability to contribute.
- Recognize that potential means nothing without performance.
- Value loyalty and consistent contribution.
- Return to the American values upon which Ford was founded, and be proud to be an American company.
- Remember that process and systems provide structure and consistency – but people produce results.
- Hire, reward and recognize rainmakers, not order takers and news reporters.
- Minimize unnecessary employee relocations that cause disruption, defections and drive up costs.

- Design and align products to meet customer demands in the marketplace.
- Maximize economies of scale in all aspects of the business on a global basis.
- Listen to the Voices: The Voice of our Employees, Dealers, Customers and Retirees.

Empowerment

- Re-launch an incentive program that rewards employees for their ideas and solutions to improve efficiency, reduce costs and grow market share.
- Decentralize as much as possible and empower employees with responsibility and accountability.
- Foster an environment where realistic goals and objectives are established and achieved.
- Have fun again and celebrate success along the way.

Mr. Carman began to pace back and forth, with a renewed energy and optimism.

"This message must immediately be communicated back to the Ford family and company leaders. They have to listen to the 'voices' around them, respond to them accordingly, and then do the right things. This is my firm belief!" concluded Mr. Carman.

There was a knock on the door, and Albert entered, holding the General's coat and hat.

"General, it's time to go. Remember, you are expected at headquarters in one hour," said Albert.

"Good luck, young man," said the General. "And remember, courage, determination and patience is the winning strategy. Follow this plan and Ford will return to greatness."

The three men marched down the hallway toward the entrance. Christopher noticed that a bright white light surrounded the General, a light so blinding that he had to cover his eyes with his hands. When he removed his hands from his face, the General had disappeared. Since it was time to go, Christopher removed his coat from the cloakroom.

"I'll see you tomorrow then, same time, same place," Mr. Carman told Christopher, waving goodbye to him from the front porch.

All along the drive home, Christopher was sorting out the information in his mind to organize for the media stories. Then his cell phone rang. It was Frank McIntyre.

"Hey, Chris, did you get the reprint of last year's news article about Ford that I dropped by your office?"

"Yes, I did, and thank you, Frank. I should have called you back sooner, but you wouldn't believe the week I've had. I've got some great news for the feature you're working on about Ford right now. I think there's a way Ford can reverse these downward trends. Let's check our schedules, set a time to get together and find a way to share this hopeful story with the public."

Frank was surprised. It sounded like Christopher was about to give him the scoop of the decade on Ford. And best of all, it sounded like a positive direction for the company.

Back at headquarters. Christopher walked toward the elevator in the parking garage, then remembered he had forgotten something in his car and went back to retrieve it. As he bent over the passenger side seat to get his papers, something fell out of his coat's inside pocket. Lying on the floor was a white envelope. Taking a second look at the coat, he realized that it was not his coat at all, but Mr. Carman's. He had taken it from the cloakroom by mistake. It was Christopher's name, however, that was handwritten on the front of the envelope. In the upper left hand corner were the initials HF. Christopher smiled. He hurried toward the exit stairs, deciding the elevator would be too slow. He couldn't wait to read what was inside. Seated at his desk, he opened the letter. The note was personally written and in a familiar tone.

From the Desk of
HF

April 6

Dear Christopher,

It's been great! I think you're on the right track and I'm impressed with your willingness to hang in there. We need good people like you to stay and help turn the company around. Thanks for investing the time with me. I enjoyed getting up to speed at what is going on at Ford. It does seem that the environment has changed drastically since I founded the company.

I'd like you to organize your notes and share them with my family and the people currently in charge of the company. But remember, however, that the basic keys to success are the same as we discussed. Explain to them that there needs to be individual accountability, compensation tied to productivity, and a balance between business and political correctness. Ford must return to an atmosphere where everyone is treated equally and where no one is discriminated against for any reason.

At Ford, managers have to become servant leaders, not self-serving leaders. We need managers to be true servant leaders, with a strong ability to listen, respond, and do the right thing at the right times. These truths were what our company was founded on. We paid a premium price for employees when we started the company, but we demanded a premium day's work. Regardless of race, gender, or ethnicity, we put everyone to work with the same pay and expected the same amount of work out of them. I think that if Ford is going to be successful going forward, the company is going to have to focus not only on the potential of an individual, but on their ability to contribute and produce in today's global marketplace.

As the founder of Ford Motor Company, I am grateful to all who have stayed the course. To them, I say, keep working hard with loyal conviction and a commitment to bettering the lives of our fellow man. I pray that God will continue to bless this great country and Ford Motor Company and keep the American Dream alive.

I will be leaving tomorrow for my journey abroad, but I will be at Fairlane Manor in the morning, preparing for my trip. I have some last-minute things to arrange, some work on the generator, and instructions for Albert. I'd like to invite you *to be my guest at the manor one last time. Why don't you drop by with your notes and join me for a cup of soybean tea?*

Sincerely yours,

Henry Ford

Henry Ford! Christopher knew it! He did not understand how the meetings of the past week had taken place, but somehow, he knew he wasn't meant to know. He was thankful that he had been granted such an incredible opportunity and was acutely aware of the responsibility of the mission. Now he had the task of carrying Henry Ford's message.

Christopher stayed up all night typing the notes for the Ford One Team Restructuring Plan. The messages were clear, powerful, insightful, and hopeful. He signed off the notes, in his usual style, with a historical quote of wit and wisdom. The company could turn around if it would listen to the 'voices,' follow the plan, and realign to the values evident in Henry Ford's original vision.

He didn't sleep a wink. It was about 5:00 a.m. when he went to the kitchen and made himself a hot cup of tea, quite out of character since he had been a coffee drinker as far back as he could remember. He smiled to himself, sipping the hot brew and looking outside the kitchen window, watching the sun rise over Dearborn. *I guess you really can teach an old dog new tricks*, he thought.

Christopher then remembered a book he owned since college — a historical collection profiling the lives of the twentieth century's greatest inventors. As if in a daze, he walked into his study and stood in front of the wall of books above his desk. *It's got to be here somewhere*, he thought, his eyes searching across the bookshelves. And then he spotted it on a shelf right in front of him. He removed the book from the shelf and sat down at his desk to read it. Scanning through the index, he was looking for the chapter on Henry Ford. Flipping through the pages, his finger stopped on what he was searching for — the events on the fateful day when Henry Ford passed away. After Christopher finished reading, he closed the book. Now, he understood. It was time to go.

"Decentralize decision-making as much as possible."
— Mr. Carman

CHAPTER FOUR

THE MESSENGER

*"You can't build a reputation
on what you are going to do."*
— *Henry Ford*

WHEN CHRISTOPHER LEFT for Fairlane Manor the next morning, the spring-like April day that had arrived at his doorstep only a few hours earlier now felt more like a cold October day as the skies filled with rain clouds and the winds swayed even the sturdiest oak trees. He hummed a song he remembered from church that past Sunday: "Will those that come behind us find us faithful?" It seemed to be a recurring chorus that he just couldn't get out of his head.

The closer he got to Fairlane Manor, the worse the weather became. It had been like that from the first day he met Mr. Carman. There, rocking on the porch and reading a book, was *Time* magazine's Man of the Century himself, Henry Ford.

Christopher's heart was racing. It's hard to explain the emotions that he was feeling that morning. Mr. Carman was indeed Henry Ford, the farmer, inventor, the common man, the *real car man*, and the founder of one of the greatest companies in the world. Christopher was excited, but he was also a little concerned that he might not be able to deliver the message to those who really needed to get it. His ability to relay the message to the Ford Family and the company leadership was not completely in his own hands. They had walls of assistants blocking direct access. It would be a challenge for sure. He also knew now that Henry Ford's cough was more than a cold. Sadness quickly overcame him.

"Mornin', Christopher," said Henry Ford, who was rocking in his chair on the porch. Christopher glanced down at the book on Henry Ford's lap. It was *Walden* by Henry David Thoreau. Today, Henry Ford was casually dressed in overalls and a worker's cap. An old farm tractor, whose engine was running, was parked at the side of the road.

"Mornin', Mr. Ford. So…you really are the 'car man'!" he exclaimed, his face beaming with excitement. Christopher held his breath, waiting for Henry Ford to say something.

Henry Ford smiled and winked at him, his eyes twinkling. Christopher held Henry Ford's coat neatly folded over his arm.

"I seemed to have taken your coat by mistake, Mr. Ford, my apologies," he offered, placing it down on the railing.

"So you have, young man," said Henry Ford with a gleam in his eye.

Henry Ford seemed peaceful today, and he wasn't coughing anymore. There was a glow about him — a certain light emanating from him.

At that moment, Albert came out of the manor carrying Christopher's coat and a tray with a pot of piping hot soybean tea and three cups and saucers. He placed the tea tray down on the wicker table and handed Christopher his coat.

"Thanks, Albert," said Christopher. Albert smiled and walked back inside the main house.

"Mr. Ford, I found the letter you wrote me. It fell out of the pocket of your coat. I stayed up all night and summarized the notes from our lunch conversations," explained Christopher, handing Henry Ford a large envelope.

"Here, sir, is the true story about the current state of the Ford Motor Company. I have included your letter to me and the strategic Ford One Team Restructuring Plan for the future of Ford. Thank you sir, thank you very much for coming back and listening to me."

"Much appreciative of your help as well, Christopher," Henry Ford replied. "And I have one more thing for you. It's a personal letter from me to those at Ford. It might come in quite handy when you reach out to the Ford Family and the company leadership."

Henry Ford handed him a letter-sized white envelope that was carefully tucked in the pages of the book on his lap. Christopher sat down and waited while Henry Ford read over his notes. When he finished glancing at them, he looked over at Christopher and smiled. He was obviously pleased.

"Well done, well done! Thank you for taking such care to record my message for the future of Ford Motor Company. Now, why don't you go ahead and read that letter that I just gave you? I hope you will do everything in your power to communicate my message to those who need to hear it."

Christopher read the letter. When finished, he looked over to Henry Ford and said, "I'm already on the case, sir, and as a matter of fact, Mr. Ford, I hope you don't mind, but I took it upon myself to invite someone from the company here to meet you this morning. He may just be the leader who can carry Ford forward with the same values and principles you founded the company on."

At that very moment, Alan Mulally, the President and Chief Executive Officer of Ford, pulled up to the front gates of Fairlane Manor in his F-150 Crew Cab. When Mulally got out of his truck, he looked curiously around him, noticing the old tractor parked to the side, and the lineup of antique cars — a Model T, a Model A, a Thunderbird, and a Mustang in the parking lot — an incredible display of famous Ford cars throughout its history.

Henry Ford carefully observed Mulally as he walked up the steps of Fairlane Manor. He stood perfectly still with his chin up and his arms to his side. Christopher was almost certain he could see tears welling up in Henry Ford's eyes.

Mulally looked surprised and a little caught off-guard. "What's going on here, Hope?" he asked, approaching the landing of the porch. *I've been here before for business luncheons and special events, but today everything looks completely different*, he thought.

"Your department didn't brief management that this was going to be a special event with period props. I was told that we were holding a press conference today at Fairlane Manor at noon, on the day of the anniversary of the passing of Henry Ford. Actually, I spent most of the morning at the Henry Ford Museum researching more on the life of Henry Ford, trying to get a better sense of the incredible man, getting some inspirational quotes and preparing a positive statement about the future of the company," explained Mulally.

Just then, thunder erupted and lightning bolted across the sky. A misty rain began to fall.

Mulally looked around the grounds and then said: "Strange… you know, when I left the Henry Ford Museum on the way here, the weather suddenly began to change. It got real foggy and the winds almost rocked my truck off the road," Mulally remarked. "My cell phone didn't work, and my car radio went wacky on me — the only thing I could get was a scratchy old Ford commercial from fifty years ago. Did somebody from your department mess with my radio? And what happened to this place? It's been remodeled or something. The cars, the old tractor — why it looks like new, and this man looks exactly like Henry Ford! It's quite a commendable effort to recapture the look and feel of a time gone by. What a great idea, Christopher! But I don't see any media trucks. Where's the press? Who else do you expect? Are we on time?"

"Well, Mr. Mulally, you are just in time. There is no one else coming, only you," explained Christopher. "Today is the anniversary of Henry Ford's death, April 7. He passed away tonight, exactly sixty years ago, here at Fairlane Manor, at 11:15 p.m., with his wife Clara Bryant Ford and his maid, Rosa Buhler, at his side. There is no press conference happening here today, and this man, who looks like Henry Ford, is, in fact, the real Mr. Carman himself, Henry Ford. The press conference idea was the best way I could get you here today and away from your busy schedule."

Mulally listened closely. Albert came back outside and approached Henry Ford.

"Mr. Ford, the power is completely out now and the generator has stopped working and the telephone is dead. You can't stay too much longer sir."

"I know, Albert. Just a few more minutes, please." Albert nodded.

Henry Ford turned to Mr. Mulally and smiled. "Welcome to Fairlane Manor. I've been expecting you. Would you like some soybean tea?"

Albert poured a cup for Henry Ford, a cup for Alan Mulally and then a cup for Christopher Hope. Mulally was beginning to understand that his invitation to Fairlane Manor today was providential.

At that very second, the grandfather clock chimed one fateful single chime. The winds picked up, bending the branches of the large old oak, and the rain fell heavier. Mulally glanced down at his watch — the hour hand was stuck at seven. *It should be noon*, he thought.

"What time do you have, Christopher?" inquired Mulally. His watch was his only link grounding him to reality. Christopher looked at his watch.

"Well, in present time it should be noon, but in history, where we are, it's seven o'clock. It's the seventh of April, sir."

Mulally stood still, barely blinking, and hardly breathing. He had prided himself on his logic, keen sense, and analytical ability, but there was another side to him that his family and friends knew very well — the dreamer, the adventurer, the visionary, and the spiritual man. He looked directly at Henry Ford, who smiled warmly at him and offered him his hand.

Mulally gazed a few moments at Henry Ford, his hand still in Henry's, and seemed to begin to come to terms with who was standing before him. Christopher noticed a gleam beginning to sparkle in Mulally's eyes. Mulally was buying into it and wasn't sure why. It just felt so right. Somehow he knew he was supposed to be there. He knew this from the first day he became the leader of Ford.

"You know, Mr. Ford," said Mulally. "When I stopped at the museum on the way over here today — walking through the rooms and exhibits, I felt great — excited and energized. I felt like a youngster again, wanting to explore, invent something, and discover something new and different. I felt happy and confident."

Henry Ford nodded and then replied: "I always said that when you can't handle events, let them handle themselves. And you know what Will Rogers once said — 'even if you're on the right track, you'll get run over if you just sit there.'" Henry Ford's signature humor always seemed to have perfect timing. He knew how to bring people together.

"You are one of my all-time hero's, Mr. Ford," remarked Mulally. "And I want you to know that I take very seriously and respectfully the responsibility of my leadership and my accountability to you and the principles on which you founded the Ford Motor Company," Mulally continued, his voice lowering to a whisper and his thoughts racing as the incredible encounter with history began to really sink in.

"As you know, Mr. Mulally," replied Henry Ford. "I can't stay much longer. This is the day I left many years ago, but it seems like only yesterday. It's funny how everything changes, yet everything stays the same. Tried to get that generator Edison gave me to work, but to no avail. Got pneumonia from this nagging cough that I just couldn't kick. I knew there was trouble down here so I came back for a visit. I was fortunate enough to come across Christopher Hope — who has been meeting with me every day for the past two weeks. He has a sincere interest in seeing the company turn around. Christopher told me quite a bit about the company's present-day condition, many things which perhaps you may not be aware of just yet. In turn, I have shared with him my perspective on how I think company leaders should respond going forward. This company was founded on my vision, yet I realize that another true servant leader could take that vision, tailor it, and carry it to the next level. From what Christopher has told me, you could just be the person to do that. Please take the time to read the notes that he has prepared from our meetings. You'll know what to do."

Mulally stood face-to-face with history and face-to-face with himself. Christopher reached out his hand to Henry Ford for a final good-bye.

"Sir, you introduced me to some of the greatest people to have ever walked the earth, who came back to set the record straight, and I will always remember everything you shared with me. I promise to communicate the message that the future of Ford and America relies on our ability to return to the basic values and principles this company and our country were founded on," said a misty-eyed Christopher.

Henry Ford smiled and shook Christopher's hand, patting him on the back. And then he turned to Mulally.

"Sometimes, Mr. Mulally, in order to go forward, you have to go back. As Will Rogers used to say — 'Rumor travels faster, but it don't stay put as long as truth.' There is a difference between signing your name on the back of a check as an employee versus having your name on the front of the check as the one responsible for funding all those checks. My name is still on the front of every check, and I take that very seriously! And my signature is on every vehicle we make, right in the center of the oval. Oh, and in case they haven't figured it out yet, tell them that the world is not an oval, it's round!"

Mulally smiled and nodded in agreement.

The three men sat down in the rocking chairs. Christopher handed Mulally his copy of the notes he had typed, and they sat quietly and waited while Mulally gave them a quick look. When Mulally turned the last page of Christopher's notes, he looked directly at Henry Ford and said, "You know, business can take very cruel turns unless it learns from history. It's important that we take the time to look in the mirror and see where we really are so we can be honest with ourselves about going forward."

On the very last page, Christopher had signed off the document with an inspirational quote of wisdom. It was by Booker T. Washington, and it read:

*"Success is to be measured not so much by the position that one
has reached in life as by the obstacles which he has overcome."*

Mulally sat back, quiet and reflective. He seemed to have lost track of
time, and when he looked up toward the rocking chair where Mr. Ford
had been only a few minutes before, it was empty. He glanced over to
Christopher who was leaning on the porch's railing and waving off into
the distance.

Looking out over the porch toward the entrance of Fairlane Manor
was Henry Ford, sitting high in his old tractor. He waved back to Christopher and Mulally and called out, "Hey, fellas, I just might check back with
you from time to time to see how things are going!" With a final tip of the
hat and a wave of the hand, Henry Ford slowly drove away, meandering
down the winding road and disappearing into the distance.

The parking lot was empty now; all the antique cars had disappeared.
Rays of warm sunlight broke through the clouds and shined down on
Fairlane Manor. Mulally looked at his watch, which was now working
fine, and the time said it was noon on the button. Albert was gone, and
everything was back to normal.

Christopher reached into his coat pocket and took out the envelope
that Henry Ford had given him only moments ago. He handed it to Mulally.

"There is one more thing I'd like to share with you, sir. Henry Ford
handed this to me before leaving on his journey and asked me to give it
to you for the company's leaders and the Ford family. It's written on his
personal letterhead and signed by him." Mulally's heart raced again. His
hand slightly trembled as he opened the doors of history and read the
handwritten letter signed by Henry Ford:

From the Desk of
HF

April 7

To Whom It May Concern,

I thought I told you everything you needed to know, but you didn't always listen.

I founded this company on certain values. I gave you the values and principles that I lived my life by. I gave you the vision and principles to ensure your success — you lost your focus. I anticipated this might happen if you didn't listen or learn. I thought you understood that money alone has never solved problems. You have lost touch with reality and with the people you are privileged to serve.

Please read the notes which Christopher Hope has recorded for you from our recent conversations. Take them to heart and please act on them. They will help realign your vision and get you back onto the road of success. I am certain that Ford Motor Company will thrive again if we get back to the basics and do the right things at the right times.

Oh, by the way, if you are still looking for the other $20 million of mine that nobody's found yet, well, here's an excellent incentive and compensation for a well-earned reward.

Before I passed on, I gave those $20 million to a trustee to invest, more than eighty years ago. Today, it has an estimated worth of over $40 billion. I had anticipated that this might happen in the future, so I created this account. I have given the trustee information to Christopher Hope.

You know what Will Rogers used to say — "Don't gamble. Take all your savings and buy some good stock and hold it till it goes up, then sell it. If it don't go up, don't buy it."

Sincerely yours,

Henry Ford

Mulally carefully folded the letter and placed it into his coat pocket. He walked over to Christopher who was still leaning on the porch railing looking out into the distance down the road where Henry Ford had been only moments before.

"How did you meet him?" asked Mulally.

"My car quit running. I was stranded, lost, and had absolutely no direction. He rescued me. Sounds crazy, doesn't it?" he explained.

Mulally put his arm around Christopher's shoulder, and the two men looked out from the porch far into the distance. "Well, Christopher, it just might take some crazy ideas and a lot of hard work to turn our great company around!"

As they looked out over the beautiful gardens of Fairlane Manor, the rain stopped and a magical rainbow reached out across the clearing skies. In the far distance, they could see Ford's world headquarters right under the rainbow. Christopher Hope and Alan Mulally looked at each other and smiled.

"Sometimes the things that really count can't be counted."
— *Mr. Carman*

CHAPTER THREE

THE RETURN TO GREATNESS

"Enthusiasm is the yeast that makes your hopes shine to the stars. Enthusiasm is the sparkle in your eyes, the swing in your gait, the grip of your hand, the irresistible surge of will and energy to execute your ideas." — Henry Ford

*I*T SEEMS LIKE *only yesterday,* Christopher thought, glancing at the date on his computer screen, reflecting over the incredible historical sequence of events that had unfolded since his last meeting two years ago with Mr. Carman at Fairlane Manor.

He was excited that Alan Mulally and the Ford management team were aggressively implementing the Ford One Team Restructuring Plan that Mr. Carman provided to Christopher before his final departure.

Once again, it was time for the Ford public relations department to issue what had become an annual press release as a memorial for company founder Henry Ford. April 7th was approaching quickly, in fact, in only a few days.

The meetings with Mr. Carman and other historic figures at Fairlane Manor continued to provide fond memories, but so much had happened since the 'Restructuring Plan' had been delivered to Alan Mulally. Ford's leadership team worked swiftly and tirelessly to restructure the company, positioning it to compete more successfully in a global environment. The engineering department ran at warp speed, designing new vehicles and refreshing every vehicle in the Ford line-up. Shared vehicle platforms were the new norm, since Ford leaders, armed with the right values, were totally focused on the products. Mulally tore down the fiefdoms that were legendary at Ford and transformed the company into a truly global corporation. He began regular Thursday morning meetings with his senior management, where the only real sin was hiding the truth. Simply put, it meant that successful products in one part of the world could be adapted to other markets — something that never happened before. The introduction of the 2011 Ford Fiesta into North America is a great example of what's on the horizon under Mulally's leadership.

If this turnaround were to occur, Mr. Carman said that it would have to be product-driven. Christopher recalled Mr. Carman's passionate message, stressed in all their meetings since then: "It's all about the product, the right product at the right time." It was clear that Mulally had gotten the message from Mr. Carman's notes. Surely Mr. Carman would smile if he were here today.

A leading consumer's magazine reported that 95 percent of Ford products made the 'recommended buy list' for the first time in the history of Ford Motor Company. One headline read, "Ford outscores Asian rivals," with a sub-headline that read "Ford secures its position as the only Detroit automaker with world-class reliability." Not only did Ford now hold the top spot in initial quality for having the fewest number of defects of any full-line auto manufacturer, but Ford could now claim excellence in long-term reliability. Ford's quality results disproved a long-held belief that only Asian manufacturers could lead in long-term durability and reliability. As a matter of proof, Ford Fusion now ranked higher than the top-selling Toyota Camry and Honda Accord in the family sedan segment. Ford had clearly separated itself as a leader once again, just as Mr. Carman envisioned.

Mulally and the engineering team at Ford streamlined its platforms significantly — reducing them to a couple of dozen. Commonality of platforms on a global basis allowed the company to leverage economies of scale on the parts involved, providing cost savings as well as quality improvements. This contributed to the simplicity of the product and reduced the number of suppliers Ford partnered with. Efficiency increased, as did mutual profitability. In retrospect, Christopher could hardly believe that Ford, a company more than 100 years old, had made over 100 major changes in just two years. It was clear evidence that when you have leadership committed to fundamental principles, things can be turned around astonishingly fast.

Christopher was proud of the Ford family for their unwavering dedication to the restructuring of the company. Many leaders have a difficult time passing the reins on, but for Bill Ford, it seemed very natural.

Not only did he relinquish the reins, but he also rallied the full support of the family behind Mulally. A great-grandson of the founder himself, Bill Ford had the wisdom and courage to select Mulally as President and CEO. The company, for the first time in its storied history, went outside the auto industry for a chief executive, hiring him from Boeing. Rumor has it that Bill Ford felt so strongly about Mulally joining Ford that he called then-President George W. Bush and asked him to give Mulally a little encouragement to accept Ford's offer. The phone conversation was simple: "Not only does Ford need you, sir, but America does too."

Bill Ford and Alan Mulally became the perfect partners to get the company back on track. Christopher knew that Mr. Carman would be proud of the leadership team running Ford now.

For the Ford family, the investment was far more than a financial commitment; it was an emotional commitment. The Ford family had always been one of the company's greatest assets. A recent news article indicated that the value of the family's special-voting shares had hit an all-time low, dwindling to a value of around $140 million from $2.2 billion in 2005. But rather than splinter, the family rallied and agreed to required sacrifices including a canceled dividend, which alone cost the Ford family members tens of millions of dollars.

Christopher looked around his office, eyeing the clutter of newspaper articles, magazine stories, press releases, editorials, memos and reports — a blizzard of automotive news from around the world. Sinking into the sofa, he sifted through the ocean of press clippings on the coffee table, hundreds of them, it seemed. He reviewed each of them.

One recent editorial evaluated the credentials of the newly appointed car Czar and the automotive task force. The commentary said that if one examined the combined automotive experience of the Czar and the entire automotive task force under a microscope — not much there. That didn't seem to matter to Washington's politicians. America was putting the future of the automobile industry in the hands of inexperienced drivers. Christopher didn't understand why the news media, which usually covered the automobile industry in great detail, was ignoring this issue. Had there ever been a time in history when the power to control an industry was given to people with virtually no industry experience? To people who were not elected or approved by any government body? It did not make sense. One out of every seven people in the United States worked directly or indirectly for the automotive industry, and novices were now in charge!

"Czar, car Czar!" Christopher exclaimed out loud. *What came after the Czars in history... let's see, there was Marx, Lenin, Stalin, Hitler, Mussolini.... he* thought to himself. *If it's a joke — it's not funny! I wonder what Mr. Carman would say about all this.*

He was certain that the country's founding fathers were rolling over in their graves knowing that non-elected Czars were running the U.S. government and many private industries. It was morally, socially and politically contrary to everything that America stood for. History had proved that the Czar system in Russia and communism, which followed in the Soviet Union, didn't work, yet it seemed to be the flavor of the day in America! Not only was there a car Czar appointed, but Czars for other industries were appointed as well.

Flipping through a dozen more articles, Christopher sat down at his computer again, staring at a blank document as he tried to write a new memorial message. *Focus, focus, focus,* he repeated to himself. The task of writing the annual release was very personal. For Christopher, this statement was one of the most important messages Ford would communicate to its audiences during the entire year. His fingers lay silent on the keyboard as the memories of his extraordinary meetings with Mr. Carman rolled by like a wonderful movie running through his mind.

Christopher leaned back in his chair, closing his eyes. He recounted the blur of events that had transpired since Mulally returned to his office the day after their last meeting with Mr. Carman. The Ford team had immediately begun work on the Restructuring Plan. From time to time, Christopher would pull out a copy of his notes and the Restructuring Plan for review. He was proud of Mulally for following the plan, which was gaining great traction. One by one, he reviewed his previous discussions with Mr. Carman and his important friends.

Mr. Carman's friends came back to set the record straight about leadership, brand management, engineering, diversity, compensation, unions, globalization, and a vision for Ford and America. With their message in the plan, the senior leadership team led by Mulally, Mark Fields and Jim Farley were able to instill a level of confidence that hadn't been felt by employees and dealers in a very long time. *Some say adversity builds character,* thought Christopher, *but in this case, adversity was actually revealing character.*

Ford was now on track with the 'Way Forward' plan that Fields had originally designed prior to Mulally's arrival at Ford. This, along with the turnaround plan implemented by Mulally wasted no time in accelerating positive changes. Mulally's turnaround plan outlined strategic viability and confronted critical issues facing the automotive industry. It communicated Mulally's strategy to transform Ford with people working together as a lean, global enterprise in automotive leadership. It detailed the importance of restructuring to operate profitably at the current demand and changing model mix, including several important areas such as accelerating development of products that customers wanted and valued, financing the overall plan, improving the balance sheet, and working together in harmony as one team.

The long term goal was to deliver a more exciting, viable and profitable Ford. The company was actively engaged in listening to customers, dealers, employees, the UAW, suppliers and retirees, without taking their eye off the competition. All these elements of the plan were crucial to Ford's success.

Ford's leadership was challenged to leverage its assets to borrow billions, focus its resources on the Ford brand, and sell off brands and operations like Jaguar, Land Rover, Aston Martin, Hertz, EasyCare, and others.

Continuing Ford's current global integration strategy was vital for success. Leadership steadfastly streamlined and stabilized Ford — right-sized the company and the dealer network and continued a product-led resurgence with new 'best in class' models in quality, fuel efficiency, safety and value. Clear progress on fuel efficiency and production of new fuel efficient cars was integral. Continuing dealer consolidation efforts was crucial, as the company made significant progress working directly with dealer partners to right-size the distribution network, particularly in multipoint metro markets. At the same time, the company communicated clear and consistent marketing messages such as 'Drive One,' 'The Ford Difference' and 'Why Ford, Why Now?'

Aggressively growing the Quick Lane network yielded incremental service share and revenue growth; this quick service solution filled the void for orphaned owners due to the dealer consolidation and attrition in the market place. Not only were they producing profits from the increase in parts sales, but Quick Lane generated the all important traffic that dealers vitally need on their dealership campus.

Even as the flurry of positive activity continued at Ford, the economic environment in America and around the world was changing at an even quicker pace. While Ford was engaged in its turnaround, rumors began to stream out of Detroit that General Motors was in titanic trouble and taking on water incredibly fast. Their failure to make necessary adjustments over the years made it look increasingly difficult to turn that ship around. Across town, Chrysler was in similar trouble.

The front page of a Detroit paper had said it best: 'Without government assistance, General Motors was sure to fail. Chrysler was offered to the largest bidder but nobody was stepping forward to rescue them. It appeared that GM's only hope for the future was a government bailout program.' Not only was GM moving into bankruptcy, but a horse race was developing between GM and Chrysler to see who could get there first.

Dealer relations issues at Chrysler were swelling over. Chrysler and Dodge vehicles weren't selling. Without viable products, a company could not survive, pointing towards the future doom of Chrysler. In a panic move, and on the advice of the new automotive task force, Chrysler sent 800 letters to loyal franchise dealers, telling them that their services and dealerships would no longer be needed and giving them 60 days notice to find another business.

This was not the dealer relationship that Mr. Carman had in mind when he developed Ford's franchise system years ago. The backlash from these 800 letters would affect at least 800 communities. This letter would put over 40,000 people out of work in an economy that couldn't afford additional unemployment. *The dismantling of the dealership franchise agreement was like pulling the plug in the bathtub,* thought Christopher, *Chrysler was spinning 'round and 'round, and disappearing down the drain.*

Meanwhile, the largest insurance company in the world, driven by greed, lack of accountability and mismanagement, had put the insurance industry in turmoil. The U.S. government was desperately trying to stabilize the financial markets. Without stabilizing insurance companies, they claimed, the world markets would be at risk.

Rather than speaking out against bad decisions by their elected officials and protecting the American Dream, too many Americans appeared more interested in what movie stars wore and who won the latest football game. Christopher wondered what the founders would think of the current situation in America.

Most Americans, it seemed, had forgotten what the founders had in mind — not everybody getting the same size of share — but everybody receiving an equal opportunity to work hard to earn a share. He was reminded of lines from a great book he had recently read called *The 5000 Year Leap*:

> *The Founders also warned that the only way for the nation to prosper was to have equal protection of 'rights,' and not allow government to get involved in trying to provide equal distribution of "things."*

He remembered that the book, written more than 25 years before, warned against exactly what the current politicians were doing, and that it meant doom to the U.S., as surely as it happened to the Roman Empire.

The economic landscape was changing at an alarming rate. Christopher felt confident that the Ford restructuring plan was being executed properly, but he hoped his friends at other automotive companies would be spared from pain. He wished that he could meet with Mr. Carman one more time to share his concerns and ask his advice — this time to save America. He knew that Mr. Carman's timeless wisdom would provide advice and comfort.

While some of his friends discussed the potential collapse of the insurance industry, they were equally fearful of instability in the other parts of the financial markets: banking and housing. The banking industry was an integral part of the automobile industry. Without a stable financial system, automobiles could not be financed. Sales of large ticket items such as homes and automobiles were directly tied to the availability of credit; a stable financial environment was essential to a stable automobile industry.

Christopher recalled a recent press article on Cap and Trade, proposed legislation supposedly designed to protect the environment but would restrict American business and cause the loss of even more jobs. It ignored the fact that other businesses around the world would not change the way they conducted business, therefore yielding negligible improvement for the world's environment. America already had the most stringent emissions laws in the world; the rest of the world was not going to change theirs. The Cap and Trade legislation placed all the burden of fixing the environment on America. which could not afford the loss of more jobs.

Cap and Trade legislation would handicap American businesses while benefiting foreign manufacturers who were not paying the costs. Not only would the average American family have to pay an additional $3,000 per year in energy costs, the burden on an already struggling automotive industry would be billions. All this in the name of global warming, even though research has shown for several years that the earth has been in a cooling cycle. Common sense points to being responsible, but not going overboard with punitive actions against American businesses.

Christopher understood that Ford operated in a global environment and that proposed Cap and Trade legislation would surely put American businesses at risk and at a competitive disadvantage, assuring that millions more jobs would be flooding out of America to regions that weren't restricted by Cap and Trade. Christopher worried that America was headed down the wrong path. It looked more and more each day as if politicians were leading the United States toward socialism, or worse yet, Marxism or fascism.

The public and private sectors continually confused activity with accomplishment. One article he read in a national newspaper called General Motors 'Government Motors' when GM emerged from bankruptcy after a landmark $50 billion dollar U.S. federal government bail-out. The free enterprise system was abandoning the very things that made it work — opportunity, accountability, personal responsibility, and independence. On top of GM's woes, Chrysler's bailout was even worse. After accepting billions from the taxpayer bailout, the U.S. allowed 15 percent of Chrysler to be acquired by the foreign automaker Fiat, for nothing — *zero* dollars.

Ford had been offered bailout money — a fat carrot, but Ford had chosen to stick with their own plan. Rather than a bailout, Ford rolled up their sleeves — just as most hard working Americans do — and began to work it out. The Ford family and leadership team came together in an effort to save Ford and the country's free enterprise system. They relied on their own resources to turn Ford around, not a taxpayer-funded bailout.

The family assembled to discuss the current situation facing Ford and America. They reviewed all options in the face of a government bailout. They could have taken the bailout or abandoned ship at any time and sold out to national or foreign interests. But Bill Ford and the family's commitment extended far deeper than their pockets; it went to the heart and soul of what it meant to be an American. The Ford family, along with Mulally, wanted to keep living that legacy and decided to reject the bailout and keep fighting for the American dream.

Energized by excitement and enthusiasm for the future of Ford, but concerned about the downard turn of America, Christopher stood up from his chair and paced. He hadn't slept well lately. Around and around the room he walked, close to the walls, as if from his peripheral vision he might discover something different, a new angle that he hadn't seen before, something to reveal a truly inspired message. Yes, he knew the message needed to be hopeful and exciting from a Ford perspective. However, he didn't want to write a Ford infomercial, a self-congratulatory press release, while so many were struggling and suffering. He certainly couldn't explain to the world that Mr. Carman, Henry Ford himself, had actually come back from the hereafter with his friends to set the record straight and provide Ford and the world a strategic restructuring plan. Or could he? As a spin doctor *par excellence* in the world of public relations, Christopher learned a long time ago that often people's perception of reality takes precedent to reality itself. But he had also learned that you always have to do the right thing, and that meant being honest and accountable to your actions and words.

The truth was that Alan Mulally had taken his assignment to heart and was proving to be the leader that Mr. Carman hoped he would be. The new servant leadership management model employed by Mulally, Fields and Farley, along with the Ford family's commitment to legacy and the American Dream, had been desperately needed and was having a positive impact. Much work still had to be done, and the uncertainties and uncontrollables of the future, were foremost on Christopher's mind.

Christopher read an article by a British journalist friend, that showed the difficulty Ford was having getting their institutional banking application reviewed, while Chrysler and GM applications were expedited and approved in record time with no resistance. Clearly, this provided GMAC an edge over Ford Motor Credit in the automotive financing arena. This also allowed the GMAC portfolio to be evaluated differently, giving them an automatic higher rating and lower interest rates, which translated into market share gains at the expense of Ford and other companies who were trying to do the right thing. This positioning had given GMAC an unfair advantage; part of the 'We will not let GM fail' policy that the administration adopted at the onset of the bailouts. The article continued with information about the legislation that was approved quickly to give a higher credit rating to these institutional banks, as well as any of the bailout banks, so that they could borrow money on the world market at a significantly reduced rate. Meanwhile, Ford and others that did not take the bailout money were left to fend for themselves, again being unfairly disadvantaged by doing the right thing by not taking taxpayer money.

Christopher sat back down, placing his head in his hands. He needed to get away — to think about things. It was all connected somehow: the founder's legacy message, the dramatic leadership turnaround at Ford, the socialist-leaning agenda of the current American government, the potential collapse of free enterprise.

Suddenly, the theme of this year's Henry Ford's memorial press release came to him. The blank white document on his computer screen now had a title as his fingers typed 'A Strong Ford = A Strong America = A Strong World.'

A random ray of sunlight broke through the threatening rain clouds hanging over Dearborn, opening a spot of a vibrant Ford blue sky. Like a laser spotlight on a dark stage, a golden sunbeam shone directly on a tall pile of press articles, magazines, and pile of papers on the corner of Christopher's desk. He thought it odd how the light seemed to shine only on that corner space, and nowhere else in the room.

Dust particles danced playfully in the sunbeam. As his eyes glanced over the pile, he noticed, at the very bottom, a large hardcover book protruding out. The coffee table book was the foundation on which the pile of papers sat; it was amazing that the whole tower of paper hadn't tumbled down. He removed the papers and magazines atop the book and smiled to himself as he gently smoothed his hand over its cover, opening up the book to an inscription dated April 7, he read: "To Christopher Hope. Thanks for having the courage to do the right thing. Remember what Mr. Carman said, 'If you do the right thing, at the right time, with the right motivation, you will get the right results. But even more importantly, you will earn the right to expect others to do the same.' This is the fundamental principle of The Ford One Team Restructuring Plan. Best wishes, Alan Mulally."

Mulally had purchased the book at the Henry Ford Museum on April 7, when he went there in search of inspiration, prior to his meeting with Mr. Carman at the manor. He offered the book to Christopher as a memento of what they had shared together at Fairlane. The book on the Henry Ford Museum featured all its exhibits, celebrated America's inventions, ingenuity and innovations, and highlighted the historical contributions made by Henry Ford and the significant role and contributions of Ford Motor Company.

He flipped through the pages and came upon a chapter about the Fairlane Manor, with photos when it was first built and how it looks today. He felt a tremendous personal connection between the Henry Ford Museum and Fairlane Manor, as he recalled how he, like Alan Mulally, thought that a drive to the Henry Ford Museum would inspire him. He contemplated how that providential trip to the museum took him on detours far away from his original destination into another place and time. He recalled his meeting with a stranger on a country road who brought him to Fairlane Manor, where he learned that history wasn't entombed in exhibits or dusty archives, but alive in the present as we live the legacies and continue the dreams.

All week, Christopher had been considering taking a drive out to Fairlane, but kept pushing the notion out of his mind. Now, though, he thought perhaps that random ray of sunlight was a sign. Glancing at his watch, he saw that it was approaching noon. *I wonder what time it is at Fairlane Manor? Heck, why not. I'm hungry. I think I'll go for a ride,* he thought.

Christopher packed up his briefcase with his laptop computer, notepad and pen, a copy of the restructuring plan, last year's memorial press release and news articles. The weather was sunny outside his window now; the stormy weather had passed. A brilliant midday sun shone over the Detroit skyline.

He buzzed his assistant. "Joy, can you please see if you can get me a lunch reservation at Fairlane Manor? Yes, today, and I'll be dining alone. Can you also request, if possible, a quiet place for lunch? I should be there at noon and plan to spend the afternoon at the manor to write this year's memorial press release… Yes, we will send out the release as usual, at 7:10 a.m. on the 7th, right before the markets open. It well may be one of the most covered releases on the wire and will be scrutinized by everyone. We have a universal message to communicate this year about the return to greatness for Ford, for America and the world. I'm shutting off my cell phone, and will check in with you on the way back. Just take messages, please. I'll be off the radar screen this afternoon. Thank you, Joy."

It might have been butterflies of anticipation or just pangs of hunger fluttering around in Christopher's stomach, but the drive to Fairlane Manor was unusually smooth. He looked around. No traffic, no detours or roadwork, just a clear Ford blue sky and smooth sailing down a newly paved road, straight ahead to what was once the home of Henry Ford and where the return to greatness had begun just two years earlier.

"There's no limit to what a team can accomplish as long as they don't mind who gets the credit." — *Mr. Carman*

CHAPTER TWO

MY BELOVED COUNTRY

"Life is a series of experiences, each one of which makes us
bigger, even though sometimes it is hard to realize this.
For the world was built to develop character, and we must learn
that the setbacks and grievances which we endure help us
in our marching onward." — Henry Ford

CHRISTOPHER DROVE UP slowly through the entrance gates of Fairlane Manor and followed the signs to the visitors' parking. Tears filled his eyes. Every time he approached the manor since his visits with Mr. Carman, he would choke up. The parking lot was crowded with tour buses with license plates from all over the U.S., a true patriotic mosaic. The estate was buzzing with folks coming and going in and out the front doors. Groups with tour guides were walking the grounds. The trees were budding and the air was fresh. The sun shone down on Fairlane Manor as a warm spring breeze blew gently; everything had a quality of new spring life.

He walked up the limestone stairs and glanced around the front porch and into the faces of strangers, looking by chance to find a familiar face or two. His heart skipped a beat when he noticed a Model T parked in front. A crowd of high school students gathered 'round as an older gentleman, wearing a utility apron and looking like a technician, was giving a talk about the car. As Christopher entered the manor, a warm feeling enveloped him. He stopped in front of the grandfather clock, a tall handsome fellow, and for Christopher, the passageway to the past. Looking up into the face of father time expecting to be recognized, the gong struck noon on the dot, bellowing out a happy crisp chime.

He glanced down at his watch which was perfectly in sync with the old clock. Although quite satisfied with it being noon in current day, in his mind's eye, he could still hear in the distance the faint echo of the clock's subsequent chimes from a more melancholy time.

"Do you have a reservation, sir?" asked the young friendly hostess at the podium.

"The name is Hope, Christopher Hope. I believe I have a reservation for noon and I seem to be exactly on time," he smiled, pointing up to the grandfather clock.She flashed back a friendly smile.

"You certainly are on time, Mr. Hope," she replied. Christopher popped his head around the restaurant door and peeked inside the crowded dining hall. "Expecting someone, sir?" she asked.

"Oh, no. Just looking," he replied.

"I see you will be dining alone today and we have reserved a quiet place for you to work this afternoon, which your assistant requested when she called this morning," the hostess said, looking down at the reservation book.

"Sir, there's a note next to your name. Let's have a look here. It says that the boss's library has been reserved for you," she said.

"Oh, I don't need an entire library. There must be a mistake. Somewhere at the back of the restaurant would be just fine. I'm all by myself and I wouldn't want to…" But before he could finish, a waitress appeared in serving attire, in costume of the manor, not in the clothing style of today. She was well on her way and hurried down the hallway and motioning Christopher to follow her. They arrived at the library's large mahogany doors.

"Come on in, Mr. Hope. Please make yourself at home. Your waiter, who tends to the library and other private rooms in the estate, will be here shortly to serve your lunch. It's a fixed house menu this week. Chefs' surprise. I'm certain you'll like it," she quipped.

"That was very kind of the boss to offer the library to me today," Christopher remarked.

"It's a special week around here, you know, it being the April 7th anniversary and all, and management thought it would be nice to open up some of the private rooms for special guests to let the sunshine in, so to speak," smiled the waitress as she fussed around the room making sure everything was in order.

"Mr. Hope, have you visited the library before?" she asked.

"Yes, I have, several times, but never dined in here," he responded.

"It's authentic to the period in furniture and décor," she explained. "It was one of the rooms of the original house which the Ford grandchildren protected from being auctioned off after Clara Ford passed away. There are certain rooms in the manor which were preserved entirely — a personal wish of the missus which the family respects till this day. Sorry to talk your ear off."

"Not at all. You seem to have a special connection to Fairlane Manor. Have you worked here a long time?" Christopher asked, trying to put an age on an ageless face.

"I never get tired of working here. Yes, I've been in the residence's service for quite some time — since I was a young girl," she blushed. "My great-grandparents were homesteaders and the original owners of Molly's farm down the road a piece," she stated proudly. "Many famous people stayed here at Fairlane, you know. Mr. Ford was a worldly man, and yet simple, down to earth. He never put on airs or made you feel lower or less than him. See that wingback chair — the well worn leather one — that was Henry Ford's favorite chair. He spent so many hours in this library, especially in the later years," she pointed out. "The library is used quite often for special dining and meeting occasions and this is the boss's favorite room in the residence."

"Wow, what a treat! If you insist that I'm having my lunch in here, then please thank your boss for me, that's just over the top. It is really cool, especially since the reason I came here today was to write the press release for Ford's annual memorial to the founder," he explained.

The lady nodded. "I'm certain you'll find your inspiration here today, and for sure I will tell the boss, Mr. Hope, and if he is around later, I'll let him know you are here and maybe you can thank him yourself," she winked.

Christopher put his bag down on the floor and removed his laptop computer, all his papers and book and placed them on the table.

When he turned, she was gone.

Standing in the center of the room, he looked around the library. *How different it looked today,* he thought. He recalled when Mr. Carman and General MacArthur rolled out the Ford One Team Restructuring Plan on that very library table, which was stark and bare then, but today was covered with a fancy white linen cloth and fine table settings. Back then the room was cold and damp, the curtains were drawn, and the lights flickered on and off. Today the room was warm and there was plenty of light. *Maybe it was all a dream,* he wondered. But then he shook his head 'no.' There were two people who had that same dream, he and Alan Mulally and 'the dream' was turning around Ford. Both he and Mulally were now living that dream.

Birds were chirping outside the open, leaded window panes facing a beautiful flowering garden. Children's laughter could be heard in the distance. Several small vases with an assortment of freshly cut flowers were decoratively placed around the room, a historical tradition at the manor started by Clara Ford.

The bookshelves held many volumes that looked to be in mint condition. He feasted his eyes on the rows and rows of classical literature, American and world history, gardening and architecture, farming, science and technology, and culinary books. Then, he noticed an entire shelf of books written by Henry Ford himself. Not only were there books about inventions, but the inventors were represented. There were also books about the historical figures and heroes that had molded the country. As much as Henry Ford had loved engineering, he had a passion for many subjects, especially history. His library certainly reflected that.

The waitress popped her head back in the room. "Excuse me, Mr. Hope. Can I bring you something to drink before your waiter arrives?" she asked. "How about some tea? A specialty of the house," she suggested.

"Sure, some refreshing tea sounds great," he replied.

Christopher decided not to use his computer to work: he felt that it would almost be a sacrilege in a room of historical authenticity. Gathering his notepad, pen and papers, he sank into the large comfortable chair next to the window, the one which the waitress said was Henry Ford's reading chair. *If that wouldn't be inspiring, what would,* he thought. He decided to write in long hand, the old-fashioned way, opening the notepad to a clean new page, taking to the task of cursive penmanship. As he started the page by writing the word 'Ford,' he marveled in the fact that the Ford Oval and brand signature was actually Henry Ford's own signature. *The business was a personal affair and that's exactly the way it should be,"* thought Christopher.

He glanced up from his notepad and noticed what looked like a family Bible on a small table at the side of his chair, and a new book right next to it. The book's cover featured a painting of George Washington. The book had a bookmark in it, as if someone had been reading it. It told of Washington's leadership as a religious and spiritual man. Christopher opened it to the bookmark, which had a picture of the Mount Vernon Museum and Estate in Alexandria, Virginia on it, the home of George Washington.

Christopher continued reading on, looking up occasionally at the door, awaiting the arrival of his tea and his waiter. He planned to spend the entire afternoon at Fairlane for inspiration and he felt he was headed in the right direction. *What the world desperately needs,* reflected Christopher, *is to replace self-serving leaders with servant leaders — leaders who don't think less of themselves but think of themselves less.* The first President, according to the book, was a man whose religion guided his governance. Throughout his career, Washington held fast to the conviction that America's liberty and freedom was dependent on faithfulness to God's will and trust in Providence.

Suddenly Christopher sensed that someone was in the room. When he looked up, he vaguely caught the back of a man leaving, a tall African-American gentleman, impeccably dressed in formal serving attire. *Funny that I didn't hear him come in,* thought Christopher, who then noticed a large silver tray on the library table with a piping hot silver tea pot and two cups and saucers. *I guess they gave me someone else's order by mistake,* he thought, looking around for the glass of iced tea he thought he had ordered and then at the two tea cups and saucers.

Standing up from his chair, he walked to the door, popping his head outside to see if he could catch the waiter, but he had already gone. Christopher decided to pour himself a cup of hot steaming tea, but found both cups were already filled.

Christopher sat down in the reading chair by the window, taking a sip of the tea. Suddenly, the familiar tantalizing taste and aroma of soybean tea filled his senses. He sipped again and again and again.

With each sip, he flashed back to his meetings with Mr. Carman. The memories came alive; he was warm inside and more relaxed than he had felt in a long time. Sunlight streamed through the open windows, and a warm spring breeze caressed him. He was getting a bit drowsy and could barely keep his eyes open. Gazing out the window and into the garden, he momentarily focused on the figure of a little woman in a wide brim straw hat, holding a wicker gardening basket and fussing around in the rose garden. She turned towards the library window, smiling and waving his way. Overcome with a contented drowsiness, he drifted off in a blissful, sleepy daydream for a few moments.

He was startled by a commotion of voices and wheels of a cart and the clanging of dishes from down the hallway. The sounds grew louder and closer to the library. Christopher jumped up from the chair and straightened out his suit jacket and tie, feeling refreshed and energized. *Finally,* he thought, *lunch has arrived!* He closed the book he had been reading and placed it on the seat. When he turned around, he was dumbstruck.

"Sir, your lunch is served. Sorry to have made you wait so long. Thought you might enjoy a few moments relaxing in the library," smiled Albert.

I'm dreaming, he thought to himself, as he watched Albert, who had appeared out of nowhere, place two lunch settings on the library table — plates of food and another pot of piping hot soybean tea. Albert just smiled, went on with his work and when finished, left the room.

Christopher rubbed his eyes. He couldn't contain his excitement, as he stared at the elegant table and the piping hot teapot. He glanced at his watch and smiled. Noon had far past and the hour hand was fixed exactly on seven. Standing in the door, top hat and gloves in hand, impeccably dressed and looking debonair, healthy and happy, was Mr. Carman.

"I told you to keep living the dream, and now you and the Ford team are living my dream," said Mr. Carman. "Remember what our friend Martin Luther King came back to remind us: 'If you lose hope, somehow you lose the vitality that keeps life moving, you lose that courage to be, that quality that helps you go on in spite of it all.' And Christopher, you are the hope of Ford."

"You came back!" Christopher almost yelled.

"No one really leaves, as long as you remember them," replied Mr. Carman.

"You look great!" Christopher exclaimed, bursting with breathless excitement.

"Thank you, young man. I have good reason to feel great. Ford is on the road to recovery. Fine work! Fine work! But you look like you've gone through the ringer since the last time I saw you," Mr. Carman observed, raising an eyebrow. "You wanted to meet with me again?"

"Yes, sir. Ford's leadership team deserves all the credit for their hard work in turning around the company as they implement the restructuring plan. It's been a challenging time for sure. But there's trouble, sir, serious trouble, in America and in the world. We're passing through the worst economic crisis in almost a century. American politics are in peril — groups are polarized, institutions gridlocked and the current government regime mistrusted. Both political parties seemed to have lost their way. And, in Washington, the D.C. seems to stand for 'doesn't care' or 'disconnected' from the constituents. Mr. Carman, times have changed!"

"Is that right?" asked Mr. Carman.

"The politicians in D.C. are passing all kinds of legislation that Americans don't want and are rapidly moving our country to a socialist regime, or worse. Many Americans have become so complacent or so trusting of the nation's leaders that they weren't even paying attention until recently, and now our country is saddled with trillions of dollars in debt. It is incredible!" Christopher continued. "Not unlike what happened at Ford before the turnaround, our country's leaders lost touch with their constituents and have adopted approaches that are counter to the principles on which our country was founded. And, you can tell how bad these programs are — none of the politicians are willing to be subject to them!" exclaimed Christopher.

"Federal government employees, including the President and members of both houses of Congress, are exempt from Social Security. They have their own plan that is much better," stated Christopher.

"Really?" said Mr. Carman.

"And they get to vote themselves raises. It resembles more the dictatorships elsewhere in the world than the United States. No one is upholding our Constitution. Is this right?" Christopher questioned.

"No, it doesn't make common sense. Has America lost its way"? asked Mr. Carman.

"I'm afraid that it has. And there may be an underlying conspiracy with far reaching implications. Sir, we need your help" said Christopher, shaking and welling up with emotion.

"Well then, it's time for a tune-up. You know what Will Rogers would say about worrying? 'Worrying is like paying on a debt that may never come due,'" Mr. Carman grinned. "You must be starving, young man. I stayed a bit longer than expected, catching up with the neighborhood gossip at Molly's farm."

"That's okay, you're the boss," smiled Christopher, not really expecting an answer.

"The customers or clients should always be the boss," he replied. "Excuse me, son, but I gotta let the missus know I'm back home or I won't hear the end of it," winked Mr. Carman as he walked over to the library window and waved to the little lady with the wide brimmed hat in the rose garden. Clara stood up and waved back, smiling.

"Good! Now we can get down to business," smiled Mr. Carman as they sat down at the table. "But before we eat, let's say a prayer." Albert returned and refreshed their cups with more steaming soybean tea.

They spoke for quite some time. Christopher had so much to share with Mr. Carman. Christopher said he had come to Fairlane Manor today to get inspiration for the memorial press release; he showed him the updated Ford restructuring plan, and all the recent press releases and newspaper stories he had brought with him. Christopher explained all the new Ford initiatives and how they were matching their products to market needs by listening closer to the voices of customers, employees, the competition, the environment, and so on. Mr. Carman was delighted and his physical health and well being seemed to be directly connected to the company's new bill of health. They reviewed everything, charting how Alan Mulally and the Ford leadership team were getting back to basics and doing the right things.

"It looks like our plan is working," smiled Mr. Carman.

"We are making common sense common practice once again," replied Christopher. Mr. Carman liked that, fighting back a laugh and replacing it with a smile.

"I notice you've been looking at two of my favorite books," smiled Mr. Carman, glancing at the Holy Bible on the table and the other book that Christopher had been reading.

"And that's my favorite chair," said Mr. Carman, as he walked over to the winged library chair. He picked up the book that was lying on the seat, the one Christopher had been reading.

"A great man, our founder, George Washington is — a true example of servant leadership and in fact, one of the greatest leaders of all time. He was the Father of our nation and also of the American Dream. We can learn all about leadership from him and if we follow his example and wisdom, we will diagnose the ills that bedevil our nation and find the cure to what ails America and the world," Mr. Carman said adamantly.

"Don't lose my place young man," said Mr. Carman, moving the bookmark further back to the exact place it had been before.

"No sir," Christopher replied, nervously trying to fix it back to its proper place.

"There are so many great books to read and so little time. My friend, an author and publisher, the late Charlie 'Tremendous' Jones profoundly stated, 'You will be the same person in five years as you are today except for the people you meet and the books you read," said Christopher. He added, "tomorrow's leaders are today's readers."

"That's very wise. You know what Will Rogers said about that?" winked Mr. Carman. "'A man only learns in two ways, one by reading, and the other by association with smarter people.' Remember, son, we become an average of the five people we spend the most time with."

Christopher put his hands to his face and rubbed his eyes again. But Mr. Carman was still standing there as clear as day, smiling and laughing.

"Have you read Milton Friedman's book, *Capitalism and Freedom*?" asked Mr. Carman, pointing to the bookcase.

"We studied Friedman years ago at college. He was a brilliant economist," replied Christopher.

"He still is a brilliant economist. Just because he's working somewhere else, we shouldn't discount his genius. I'll loan the book to you, if you like," offered Mr. Carman.

"Thank you," replied Christopher.

Mr. Carman continued, "Friedman won the Nobel prize for economics. During his career, he advocated minimizing the role of government in a free market as a means of creating political and social freedom. He believed that the world runs best with individuals pursuing their separate interests and that the great achievements of civilizations have not come from government bureaus. He reminds us that Albert Einstein didn't construct his theory as a result of an order from a bureaucrat."

Christopher laughed.

Mr. Carman continued," And we didn't revolutionize the automobile industry that way either! Friedman said that the only cases in which the masses have escaped from grinding poverty were where they had capitalism and largely, free trade. And, if you want to know where the masses are worse off, it is exactly in the kinds of societies that depart from that; on this the record of history is absolutely crystal clear. In his own words, 'there is no alternative way, so far discovered, of improving the lot of ordinary people that can hold a candle to the productive activities that are unleashed by a free enterprise system. The countries with the most poor and oppressed citizens are dictatorships with communist, socialist, marxist or similar orientation.' And, it sounds like that is where your nation's current leaders are taking you, Christopher." said Mr. Carman.

"Wow," said Christopher. "We need guys like you and Friedman here today to help re-instill the values of limited government, to help stablize the economy, and teach us lessons from the past. 'Those who don't know the past, are destined to repeat it.'"

Mr. Carman smiled. "You know what Friedman means? Free man. And that's what he advocated — freedom. True freedom comes from the free enterprise system. Milton came from a humble background just like I did. He was a simple man, who struggled, studied and worked hard all his life to achieve great things as he lived through one of the most challenging and productive centuries in our history. And history really does repeat itself," continued Mr. Carman.

"The government bailout of the automotive industry and the threat to the collapse of the free enterprise system is not new. In 1931, the Great Depression was taking its toll on the country's economy. President Hoover moved the United States away from its previous policies of limited government and promotion of free enterprise. He believed that the decline of industry and agriculture could be stopped — that unemployment could be reversed and purchasing power restored, if the federal government would bailout the banks and railroads. Hoover modeled this after an approach used in the Great War which had seen some success. The President got approval for his plan from both houses of the Congress and they passed legislation creating the Reconstruction Finance Corporation, the RFC, with two initiatives. Congress provided it with initial capitalization of $500 million and the RFC had the power to borrow up to $2 billion to secure the survival of the large banks, railroads, farm mortgage associations, savings and loan and life insurance companies. General Motors, one of Ford's closest rivals at the time, went to the RFC for aid, which helped them in opening another new bank. Sound familiar, son?" he continued.

"On the good news of the RFC's initial 'success' in helping prevent bankruptcies, Congress pushed to extend loans to other sectors in the economy. Fortunately, it never expanded even though the administration at the time wanted it to. The law called for complete transparency and often the institutions who sought loans lost public confidence as worried depositors ran from banks seeking federal assistance. Taxes and tariffs on the American people then erased a lot of the positive impact that people initially thought the RFC had accomplished.

"Does that sound familiar?" Mr. Carman asked. "That is where the U.S. will be in a few years when taxes keep increasing to pay for those government 'stimulus' packages. But why did the RFC fail? I'll tell you why. Because its underlying premise, which was called industrial self-government, was plain out socialism.

Mr. Carman continued, "I refused to sign the automobile code of the National Recovery Administration, which stipulated that employees had a right to organize. When government has too much control, the free enterprise system doesn't work. Industrial self-government or socialism, clearly meant that segments of the economy could extend to take over other parts of the economy to work 'in harmony for the national benefit of everyone.' That could never work. Organized businesses used the National Recovery Administration to manipulate for higher prices and serve their needs. If it would have lasted, it would have created permanent unemployment and severely depressed the standard of living for most Americans.

"I argued that high wages and short hours were satisfactory to most workers in our plants. And I had serious reason to suspect that a group of international financiers were gaining control of the unions and using their influence to exploit both labor and management. Perhaps these international financiers are at play once again in America today, only the stakes seem much higher.

"When you and I had one of our first lunch meetings at Fairlane Manor, and we discussed the lack of leadership at Ford, I shared with you how in the early 1920's, Ford faced its most difficult industrial crisis. Let's review that situation again within a contemporary context, because it is precisely due to the current optimistic and resourceful leadership that Ford is getting back on its feet again.

"When General Motors came out with Chevrolet, we were producing more than two-thirds of the automobiles in America. But as their production mounted, our sales dropped. We closed plants, scrapped the Model T and redid our entire production system. We retooled our plants, retrained our workers and came out with a completely new product. Americans loved it and we expanded. Son, that's what is called industrial renovation — replacing currency with creativity.

"Ford could have really used a financial bailout in the crisis of 1921 — probably one of the most severe in history. We couldn't meet our obligations — we were short by more than half and were facing impending bankruptcy. The bankers were counting the seconds for us to walk through their doors, expecting me to go 'hat in hand' on my knees. One of the officers from a large New York bank came to see me in Detroit and offered Ford a huge bailout on the condition that a representative of the bank be appointed treasurer of Ford with full control over its finances," laughed Mr. Carman.

"Sound familiar, son? Well, he got my answer! I handed him his hat. Perhaps your administration's bailout packages, and Czar appointments with financial connections to industry, have similar strings attached — we must not be naïve.

"How did we respond to an offer they thought we couldn't refuse? We rolled up our sleeves and asked our Ford dealer partners throughout the nation to take as many cars as they could take, and asked them for cash in return, which provided the complete funds we needed to meet our obligations. Then with those funds, we purchased our own railroad and used that to cut a third from the time our raw materials and finished products were in transit. We decreased inventory of goods needed on hand for uninterrupted production and released more than that amount from capital funds into ready cash. Doesn't that sound better than selling out to a bunch of bankers or the government?

"You must be resourceful to weather the storms. I embraced two principle economic policies during Ford's incredible growth — continued cutting the cost of the product as improved methods of production made it possible, and the payment of higher wages, allowing our employees to not only share in the risks, but share in the rewards of their efforts. We strived to remain optimistic in the most challenging of circumstances. To reduce costs and cut intermediate costs on raw materials and transportation, we purchased our very own coal mines, iron mines and forests, railways, lake and ocean steamships. They were run on the Ford brand, if you will, of paying high wages to keep production high and costs low.

"By owning these industries, which were collateral for us, we were set if we ever needed them as financial security or a guarantee. We were able to control waste on all levels and be self-sufficient, maintaining our independence from 'industry self-government,' which as I mentioned, is otherwise known as socialism. That's the only way to ensure free enterprise. I think there are many dangers associated with outsourcing everything to other companies or countries. You will find some parallels and lessons in what I just shared with you. As I said, you can see that history really does repeat itself, Christopher."

Christopher took in all that Mr. Carman said. After a moment, he responded. "Sir, there really are many parallels. Right now, Ford is at a competitive disadvantage when compared to post-bankruptcy GM and Chrysler in several key areas. Just when the new 'kumbaya' era of management-union cooperation looked to be actually taking hold of the domestic automobile industry, after years marked by sheer lunacy, we are once again being reminded that common sense and 'big picture' thinking are concepts that continue to escape the UAW. Why, they just recently voted down a contract change that would put Ford back on par with GM and Chrysler. According to a recent article, one of the union dissidents who led the campaign against ratification, said 'workers made their voices heard on the top floor of Ford's world headquarters — we sent a clear message to Ford that the time for concessions are over.'

"Once again, we continue to operate with a shirts versus skins mentality, and by that I mean management versus labor — a completely archaic system of operation. The UAW membership has declined from 1.5 million in 1979 to 431,000 in 2008, primarily due to an out-of-touch, out-of-time and out-of-step model in the sobering realities of America's economic future.

"Our current labor costs are still much higher when compared to the three major non-union companies — Toyota, Honda, Nissan — and now we're placed at a disadvantage to our cross-town rivals for the first time in recent memory. That spells an end to the pattern bargaining system that has defined relations between the UAW and Detroit's Big Three for decades. Ford now faces the prospect of entering into national negotiations with the UAW in 2011 as the only automaker the union can strike, meaning Ford is likely to become the focus of any efforts to win a better contract. The article went on to say, 'the unexpectedly fierce opposition to the UAW-Ford agreement is a bad sign for the industry and the region and really enforces that negative image of Michigan and the industrial Midwest.'"

Mr. Carman selected a book from the shelf and handed it to Christopher. "There are always conflicts — internal and external. That's the nature of things. You may find what you're looking for, right here in this book. It's a collection of the founders' writings. You need to put it in a historical context when you try to understand the worries which the founders expressed.

"The answer to what ails the nation and the world today can be found in the writings of the founders. Benjamin Franklin wrote that serving in a public office was an honor and not a position of profit. And the founders believed that good government and the welfare of all people, required religion, morality and knowledge."

Mr. Carman continued. "The founders recognized that the correct role of government is to protect equal rights, and not to provide equal things. Taking from the haves and giving to the have-nots as was done in Europe during those days was not equality. They also understood the abuses of autocratic governments and believed that the majority of the people can and should abolish a government which becomes tyrannical and no longer represents the views of its people. The America they fought to establish provided equal opportunity, not a guaranteed equal share.

"Our Constitution was created to protect our people from the human nature of powerful rulers and it placed power in the hands of the people, not the governing leaders. Our founders believed in a free market economy with a minimum of government regulations, with three branches of government and checks and balances against the abuse of power. They also believed in law as a stable frame of reference for the security of its people. They understood the value of education, that a free enterprise system leads towards prosperity, and that those enviable conditions where industry and commerce prosper are also fraught with the potential of greed.

"The principles of Jefferson were not encouraging isolationism with other nations, but a separation, a peace and friendship so as not to get too meshed into foreign alliances. The founders also wisely advised that debt was destructive to freedom. Franklin said, 'Think what you do when you run in debt; you give to another power over your liberty.'

"Go back and tell them to read the founders' writings and the principles and laws which our country was founded on. The answers are there and the people will know what to do. They always do. Is it possible that an entire nation, as blessed and as brave as the United States of America, has become deaf, dumb and blind? If we break the foundation, the building will fall," Mr. Carman warned.

"About the qualities of great leadership, well, most problems come either from a lack of inspiration or a lack of information. As I mentioned before, leaders must strive to create passionate and engaged talent at all levels. Creating truly engaged workers requires a servant leadership model where leaders don't think less of themselves, they just think of themselves less. You have to develop an environment that encourages truth tellers. You must not reward "yes" men and women over those willing to rock the boat and tell the truth, even when it means radical change and is counter to your corporate culture. You have to establish accountability partners and encourage unfiltered feedback.

"A company's greatest assets are not their fixed assets, but the people who walk out the door every night, and the leader's job is to make them want to come back the next day. Hold people accountable. And beware of the CAVE people — you know them — the ones who are **C**ollectively **A**gainst **V**irtually **E**verything. They are dream destroyers — the ones who will come up with hundreds of reasons why each new idea will not work."

"I have worked with several CAVE people over the years," laughed Christopher.

Just then, a bell rang. "Oh, good," Mr. Carman said as he stood up. "Son, we're going for a ride."

Christopher's heart pounded. He suspected that a journey with Mr. Carman was going to be unlike any other. "Where are we going, Mr. Carman?" he asked excitedly.

"To see how it all began!" he exclaimed. Mr. Carman was already half way down the hall as Christopher packed up his briefcase and ran to catch up with him. Mr. Carman's voice echoed through the mansion: "Come on son, get a move on and catch up."

The rooms at Fairlane Manor were empty now; all the lunch guests and tourists were gone. The staff continued cleaning up tables, sweeping floors, and tending to all sorts of chores. Fairlane was cheerful, warm and happy, in stark contrast to earlier visits with Mr. Carman and his friends.

Passing in front of the old grandfather clock, Christopher glanced up into its face; the hour hand pointed to seven. He then checked his watch and found it also stuck on seven. Then the clock chimed seven times; Christopher shook his head and understood.

Standing on the front porch of the manor, Christopher couldn't believe his eyes. He was absolutely flabbergasted at the sight of an incredible vehicle.

"Isn't it a beauty? A friend drove it all the way to Fairlane from Mount Vernon!" exclaimed Mr. Carman. To Christopher's astonishment, parked right in front of Fairlane Manor, was the magnificent, specially commissioned, built-to-order American-LaFrance Combination Chemical and Hose Car, Mount Vernon's first fire truck, which Mr. Carman donated to George Washington's home and estate in 1923. On the front of the truck, was an American flag waving in the breeze.

"Wow! Unbelievable! It can't be. Is this the original fire engine"? he gasped.

"Sure is, son," Mr. Carman winked. "I visited Mount Vernon, home of President George Washington in the early 1920's, and I was greatly impressed by this tribute to our nation's first President. In the spirit of preserving an important icon of our nation's past, I commissioned a special chemical fire truck for Mount Vernon. The revolutionary fire truck was an essential tool in protecting Mount Vernon against its greatest threat back then — fire. The arrival of this fire engine was the beginning of our company's commitment to protect and preserve Mount Vernon and other aspects of American heritage. I was inspired by the efforts of the Mount Vernon Ladies' Association to preserve Washington's history. It gave us the vision to establish The Henry Ford Museum, documenting America's traditions of resourcefulness and innovation."

"Well, what are you waiting for young man? Climb on board!" yelled Mr. Carman.

"Where are we headed?" asked Christopher again.

"To see how it all began, son, how it all began. I want you to meet a good friend of mine. He will explain to you the significance of the American Dream," said Mr. Carman. "But first let's try to define what the American Dream really is," sighed Mr. Carman. "Go ahead, son, take a shot at it."

"Um... democracy, freedom, individual rights, to have a family, own a house, a car and grow a business, to..." and then Mr. Carman interrupted him.

"Yes, it's all about those things, but at the core of the American Dream is sacrifice and courage. Simply put, the American Dream was the same for my grandparents, my parents, for me, for my kids and grandkids and it's the same for yours. The American Dream stands for equal opportunity — through hard work. If we work hard, we can create a better life for our children and grandchildren." Mr. Carman had captured it perfectly and Christopher agreed.

Mr. Carman turned on the engine. He clanged the bell and blew the horn. Suddenly it began to snow. Larger and larger the flakes swirled down and in a few seconds time, they were caught in a whirling, blinding blizzard, circling the fire truck, 'round and 'round. Visibility was zero. The squall quickly subsided, and in the distance, Christopher thought he heard the thundering galloping of horses. Entering through the gates of Fairlane Manor were men in 18th century military outfits, slowing down as they approached the fire truck. Mr. Carman dusted himself off, jumped down excitedly to greet the guests. Christopher noticed one man in particular dismounting his horse as he smiled at Mr. Carman.

"Great to see you," said Mr. Carman. "I'm so happy you could make it, General. I'd like to you meet my friend, Christopher Hope,"

It only took a second for Christopher's knees to weaken; he began to feel a little faint as he stepped from the fire truck. He knew better than think the man was a museum guide in period costume dressed up as General Washington; why, he was in the company of the original Mr. Carman!

An aura of light surrounded the tall impressive man; he exuded magnetism unlike anything that Christopher had ever experienced. He gazed down at the man's long black military boots that extended all the way up to his knees. His eyes continued up the stately and distinguished towering figure, past a long-tailed military jacket with round gold buttons and white cuffs held two engraved gold cufflinks. A military medal was pinned on the jacket's collar and a white silk scarf was wrapped around a strong slender neck. Christopher saw the face of a man lined with years of suffering and the grace of the ages, and the most intense and piercing blue eyes he had ever seen — a face which Christopher would never forget.

"General, sir," whispered Christopher, lowering his head and placing his hand on his heart like pledging allegiance to the flag, fumbling with his hand, not knowing whether to salute or what to do.

Mr. Carman offered the General his hand which was duly returned with a robust shake.

"Gentlemen, no formalities. And young man, unless you are having a case of heart failure and require urgent medical intervention, please remove your hand from your chest and relax," smiled the General.

"Come on into the manor. Let's have some soybean tea to warm up," said Mr. Carman as they walked up the steps and into the manor. Albert was waiting for them, taking the General's hat, coat and gloves.

A splendid fire was ablaze in the library and Albert had already begun serving the guests some piping hot tea and snacks.

"I understand that you wanted to meet with me about certain issues that are placing our freedoms in jeopardy once again," said the General.

Mr. Carman turned to Christopher.

"Son, I've asked the General to join us here today to address your concerns," said Mr. Carman, with a look of encouragement to Christopher.

173

"Yes sir, General," said Christopher, fumbling for words and searching for his voice. "Leadership on all levels is being compromised in America and in the world. Greed is rampant. The states are in pain. Czars are being appointed to lead industry in America. Democracy is in peril. American people exercising their freedom of speech under the Constitution are being criticized and silenced by the government. There are public outcries against legislation being bulldozed through without proper review and participation by the people. Minority rights, under the banner of diversity, are trumping majority rights. Our Constitution, ethics and morality are being compromised. Our borders aren't properly protected. We need your help. I wish you could come back and be our leader again," said Christopher, his eyes wet with tears.

"I never left, Mr. Hope. You speak of greed. Are you of the belief that this is a modern phenomenon? States in pain? Czars in America? Democracy in peril? Sabotaging the Constitution?" questioned the General in a sharper tone.

"I believe that America needs a spiritual revolution," Christopher replied, raising an eyebrow.

"The first word of advice," General Washington responded, "is to remember that leaders are not angels but fragile human beings. Government must be harnessed within the confines of a strictly interpreted Constitution or it will destroy the very freedom it was designed to preserve. Government is not reason, not eloquence, it is force. Like fire, it is a dangerous servant and a fearful master.

"My political views were shaped more by practical experience than political theory. In the beginning, I had a vision for America. Even before the Revolution, I thought that fostering economic self-sufficiency in America would be a way of retaliating against the British. I wouldn't budge on what I believed was right or wrong and acted on what I thought."

"General, what advice would you give to our leaders today?" Christopher asked, now feeling more confident and definitely more relaxed.

"I've often said that it is the actions, not the commission, that makes the officer, and that more is expected from him, than the title. Your actions define you. The America that I helped establish faced many obstacles. We believed in a better world where everyone had the opportunity to succeed without excessive taxes by the ones in charge. With freedom comes responsibility for individuals to do the right thing. The quickest way to destroy any free enterprise system is too much government control."

The unusual spring snow picked its pace up again; the winds howled, shaking the window panes. Snow drifted up against the walls of the manor. Christopher stared into the hypnotic dance of flames in the hearth. A dreamlike golden haze of warmth and sleepiness enveloped him as the General continued to speak.

"The America we battled for has never promised an entitlement program or equal share to everyone, but it did promise to provide an equal opportunity for everyone to earn their share, and that's what has and will always make America a great nation. This motivated people to work hard; that is why we have the greatest wealth of any country in the world and the greatest number of people with wealth."

"There are many far more worthy than I who'd give anything to speak with you, sir." said Christopher.

"The doors of history are always open. In due course, tell them what I said. My views are widely communicated to anyone that wishes to seek them. It remains then to be my request that you will communicate these sentiments to our countrymen. You are a messenger, entrusted to report facts and to be honest."

The lively conversation in the library between the General and Mr. Carman was intriguing. Christopher remarked on how much George Washington and Henry Ford had in common. Both were men of practicality and vision. They had grown up on farms and held a keen appreciation and respect for the environment. *These are the kind of leaders we need in America today,* thought Christopher.

It was time for the General to go. The sun had vanished over the horizon and the stars emerged. Albert brought warmed coats and hats for Mr. Carman and Christopher as the General nodded to his soldiers waiting at the gates. Everything was now blanketed in snow except the fire truck, which gleamed in the moonlight. The flag on the fire truck rippled in the brisk northern winds.

General Washington had agreed to let Mr. Carman keep the truck for a little bit longer before returning it to Mount Vernon.

As General Washington mounted his horse, he handed Christopher a sealed envelope bearing the official insignia of Mount Vernon. Inside was a note for him, and another for Alan Mulally. After they all said their farewells, Christopher opened his note and read it; when he was done, he carefully tucked the envelope back inside his coat pocket.

Mount Vernon
Alexandria, Virginia
GW

Mount Vernon — 6 April
Mr. Christopher Hope

Dear Sir,

Please do come and visit us at Mount Vernon. I thoroughly enjoyed meeting you and listening to your concerns for our beloved country.

You will witness the Sacrifices of your Countrymen and the birth of the American Dream. Tell my courageous people this: The thing that has always set the American people apart from all others is that they will die on their feet before they will live on their knees. Above all, to return America to greatness, you must honor God and uphold the Constitution.

Remember the importance of the wisdom of the ages and that if wisdom is not to be acquired from experience, where is it to be found?

I have also herewith included a correspondence for Ford's current leader, Mr. Alan Mulally, if you would kindly give it to him on my behalf.

And please send our gratitude and prayers to Ford's leadership team and family. I am with great regard, sir, Your Most Obedient and Most Humble Servant,

G Washington

"He's the greatest leader the world has ever known," exclaimed a teary-eyed Christopher as he watched the General and his soldiers gallop through the gates of Fairlane Manor, slowly fading away in the distance. "I don't want him to leave. Why can't he come back with us and tell them himself and show them how to do things right?"

Mr. Carman smiled.

"He did his job. His work is done. It's up to you now, son," said Mr. Carman. "He showed you how, and he told you how. You just have to remember and pass it on — the legacy and the dream — one person at a time, each and every day. No guarantees, son, but there are many opportunities and chances to get the right results. Like the General said, the doors of history are always open, the books are written and waiting to be read and you are all welcome to visit with him at Mount Vernon anytime."

As the General and his soldiers faded away into the distance, afternoon light and warmth returned, melting the snow with afternoon sunlight and a spring like breeze, gently ushered in. Birds were chirping and suddenly there wasn't a flake of snow anywhere. *Time was so elusive,* he thought, *that when you are pressed for it, you barely notice the world around you. When time isn't an issue, you are vitally alive in every second.*

Mr. Carman and Christopher walked up to the fire engine.

"I should be going now, but would you mind if I sat in it one last time?" asked Christopher.

"Sure thing son, why, hop on in," laughed Mr. Carman, who also jumped into the driver's seat, with Christopher at his side.

"It's a magical vehicle, isn't it?" smiled Christopher.

"Certainly is, certainly is," smiled Mr. Carman, who clanged the bell and blew the horn.

"You know son, I heard a few things that just didn't sound right with the truck. Maybe it's the motor — probably needs a tune up. I think I'll change my clothes before it gets dark and have a look at it myself," smiled Mr. Carman excitedly, eager to get to work on it.

"Oh, I thought you might like to know that Ford is having a press conference at the museum the day after tomorrow, April 7th, in your honor," announced Christopher, proudly.

Mr. Carman smiled.

"We planned an entire founder's tribute day in celebration of your life and incredible legacy of resourcefulness, ingenuity and innovation that made Ford and America great. Mr. Mulally will meet the press and host a luncheon for some of our employees," explained Christopher. "With our turnaround, all eyes are on Ford now, watching our every move. Many wish us success and see it as critical to the state of the economy, the future of free enterprise, and maybe even our country."

"Christopher, the lesson we have learned from our visit with the General is that what is good for the company will also be good for the country and good for the world. You see, my vision for Ford was to make the world a better place, and not just to make money. While the money provides us the tools to make the world a better place, I always encouraged and demanded that Ford reinvest a percentage of all the revenues that we took in, to continue to develop America and the world, to make it better for mankind. As you know, regardless of what they say, the American Dream was the same for me when I was at the reins. That's one of the things that makes America unique. And if Alan Mulally wants to speak with me, tell him I'm around. He knows where to find me. Tell him I am proud of him, his leadership team, and all the employees of Ford Motor Company. I couldn't be more proud of my family and the way they stuck together to save Ford. They are a real team.

"I am also particularly proud of all the franchise dealers across the world and the job they've done in difficult times — to continue my legacy of providing affordable and safe transportation to the masses and for making the world a better place."

"Thank you for introducing me to General Washington, and for coming back to visit with me again," said Christopher.

"I never left. Keep living the dream, son, keep living the dream," Mr. Carman winked.

Christopher got into his car and drove out the iron gates of Fairlane Manor. "Please don't go, Mr. Carman," he said out loud, as he watched Mr. Carman waving goodbye to him in the rear view mirror.

Driving down the highway, Christopher glimpsed a spectacular rainbow arched over the interstate. He tuned his car radio to the four o'clock news. Only a few hours had passed since he had arrived at noon for lunch at Fairlane Manor. Opening up his cell phone, which was beeping with messages, he dialed his assistant, Joy.

"Hey Chris, the media's going wild looking for some scoop on the upcoming press conference on the 7th at the Henry Ford Museum. You also had a call from Mr. Mulally right after you left. I told him you were out for the afternoon, writing the memorial press release. He sounded very excited about the upcoming event at the Henry Ford Museum," Joy reported.

"Great! Can you do me a favor?" asked Christopher. "Call up to archives and ask them to pull the original Henry Ford obituary announcement written and released by the A.P. on the day after his passing, April 8, 1947. Put it on my desk, please? I may send that obituary out to the media, along with this years' memorial release. I think the media needs a shot of some good old-fashioned journalism, and a reporting of facts and figures as they happened, about how our founder was perceived and appreciated by his contemporaries in his time."

"Sure thing, Chris," Joy replied.

Then Christopher dialed his wife.

"Hi Faith! Sorry sweetheart — I had my phone off again all afternoon. No, I am not having an affair — you know you're my one and only, and besides, I tell you everything."

"Yeah. Well, your office said you were at Fairlane Manor looking for inspiration. Who did you have lunch with this time? Napoleon Bonaparte, or maybe the Dali Lama? I heard he was in town," she chuckled.

"Very funny. I thought you really believed me about my meeting with Mr. Carman and his friends," he said.

"Come on, Christopher, I want to believe you but you have to admit, it's asking someone to take a leap of faith into someone else's imagination. I'm sorry, I didn't mean to say you made it up, but… someone else's inner world of faith and dreams. You know what I mean?" she said.

"I know. As long as you listen with an open heart and mind, that's the most important thing in any relationship," he replied.

Faith was silent for a moment. "So, I'm listening. Tell me, really, who did you meet today?" she asked.

"Mr. Carman and Albert at Fairlane Manor, then George Washington," he replied.

"I see, and all in one afternoon too?" she asked, a little sarcastically.

"Yes, Faith. I know it sounds crazy. But these are crazy times."

"Take a deep breath Christopher, and relax," Faith interrupted. "You're going to have a nervous breakdown and then what good would you be — who would save the world then? We're all worried about what's happening to our country. That's what everyone is talking about — at the store, in the gym, on blogs, everywhere. America has gotten off track. But the people are beginning to speak up about having the wool pulled over their eyes by those in government. So what did your friends from history have to say about all this? No, I'm really being serious now," she urged.

"They said that only a free enterprise system could ensure all humans equal rights. They said that sacrifice was the foundation of the American Dream and to remember that's what made America great because what's good for our company is also good for our country and good for the world. They said to be courageous, keep working hard and keep living the dream."

"Wow. That's so true. I can feel their passion speaking through you. I love you, Chris and I know how hard you've been working and how your heart is breaking for America. You're worried about the kind of future we are preparing for our kids. I guess the real test of faith is believing without seeing. Some people can see things that others can't. I try to see through your eyes. Your optimism makes me optimistic, and your dedication and loyalty to your company and country makes me proud and I'm a better person for it."

"I don't know what I did to deserve you," said Christopher.

"I'm not sure what I did to deserve you either," laughed Faith.

"Ok, very funny," he replied.

"I have a husband who meets historical characters for lunch and travels with them through time and space, who wants to save Ford and the country," she chuckled. "Oh well, just a normal day in the life of Faith Hope. My mother warned me about marrying for love and to a guy whose last name was Hope." Christopher laughed and settled in for a comfortable evening at home with his wife.

The next day, Christopher finalized this year's press release — 'The Annual Memorial of Founder Henry Ford Marks the Tribute to America and Lessons in Leading in Difficult Times — A Strong Ford = A Strong America = A Strong World.'

He then sent it to Alan Mulally before shutting his computer down. The press kits were assembled, ID and media badges printed, and VIP passes prepared. Everything was ready for the founder's anniversary event at the Henry Ford Museum tomorrow morning.

"What the free enterprise system really means is that the more enterprising you are, the more free you are." — *Mr. Carman*

CHAPTER ONE

THE MAN WITH THE PLAN

*"One of the greatest discoveries a man makes,
one of his great surprises, is to find he can do
what he was afraid he couldn't do."*
— Henry Ford

ALAN MULALLY WAS so excited that he barely slept the night before. He remembered as if it were yesterday his visit to the museum two years before, for inspiration and revitalization. He remembered the incredible meeting afterwards with Mr. Carman at Fairlane Manor. After all, it was the day that Ford's return to greatness began.

Yet the troubles and worries that his countrymen and people everywhere were experiencing weighed heavy on his shoulders, despite the good news turnaround reports from Ford. The headwinds had indeed shifted and the breeze at his back felt much better, but he still wished he could meet with Mr. Carman one more time, since he had many more questions. Mulally wanted him to know how hard they had worked to continue the Ford legacy.

Ford's leader woke up way before sunrise, as he always did, wanting to get to the museum early, before the crowds arrived. In the quiet of the morning he wanted to spend some time alone, taking in the spirit of ingenuity and positive energy incubating there, just as he had done two years earlier on that providential April 7th when he first met Mr. Carman. So much had happened since then, and he was grateful. He felt that it was appropriate to have the memorial at the museum this year. Within the solemnity of the occasion, a tremendous life would be celebrated and a cherished legacy would continue.

Looking out his kitchen window, he saw a beautiful sunrise creeping up over Dearborn. He paused in memory of Ford's founder — one of the greatest men that ever lived, Henry Ford. A magnificent spring day was unfolding. He turned on his computer and was pleased and energized by this year's anniversary message, and was certain that Henry Ford would be too.

The press conference was called for eleven o'clock, and then he was hosting a lunch meeting and planned to attend all the afternoon's activities. There was still plenty of time to catch up on work. After reviewing and answering emails, going over his talking points, scanning through dozens of news articles, he was ready to go to the museum. He wanted to be there early.

I think I'll wear my lucky red tie today, Mulally thought. It was the tie he had often worn, and the one he wore on the first day he took over the reins at Ford. He grabbed his sport coat, got into his new Taurus and drove toward the museum.

When he drove up into the museum parking lot, it was oddly empty, except for an original Model T parked way far back near the exit. There wasn't a soul around and the museum lights were still out. He walked up the steps and pressed his forehead on the glass entrance door, to see if he could see anyone moving around inside. All of a sudden, through the tinted glass, he saw a security guard walking towards him. The guard smiled and waved, motioning for him to wait a moment as he pushed some buttons on a wall panel. The museum doors opened.

"Hi. I'm Alan. We're having a company event here today. Are you open yet?" he asked.

"Mornin,' sir. I'm afraid we're not open quite yet," the security guard replied, checking the time on a gold-toned pocket watch dangling from a chain on his vest. "We're not open to the public today, being a special Ford event and all, and my orders are to open the doors at 10:00 a.m."

"Oh, I'm sorry. I guess I got here earlier than I had expected. I wanted to get my tank filled with inspiration early on."

"I always liked a man who was ahead of schedule," chuckled the guard.

"No problem. I'll go have a cup of coffee and come back later," Mulally suggested.

"Nonsense," exclaimed the guard! "Come right on in, young man. I'm about to do my early morning inspection walk through. Just don't tell the boss," he quipped.

"Is that your Model T parked out there?" asked Mulally.

"It's a beauty, isn't it," said the guard.

"We just got a special historic vehicle in here early this morning, on loan from another museum; it's for the Tribute to America exhibit for today's event. Some mechanical work has been done on the motor and I've got some cleaning rags here to shine it all up," explained the guard, as he picked up a bucket filled with rags and plastic spray bottles with cleaning liquid.

"Wow, I'd love to see that exhibit," said Mulally. "It's sure going to be an exciting day!"

"I know," replied the guard. "I'd be obliged to take you on a personal tour with me as I do my morning rounds," he offered.

"Really? That's very kind of you. Why, you must know the history here like the back of your hand, lots of trivia and little known facts," exclaimed Mulally.

"You bet your bottom dollar I do, son. If you want to know what America is all about, this is the place!" he replied.

"You're so lucky to work here," said Mulally.

"I guess you could say we're both working in good company," laughed the guard. "I never tire of seeing the innovation and ingenuity of the people of this great country. The real resource and industry of this nation, what makes America great, is spelled out in the struggles of America from our beginning and right up to the present. Greatness comes from struggles, young man, not laziness and easy street," he exclaimed, moving along quickly down the hallway.

"Let's get moving, son. Follow me, we've got lots to see and not a lot of time. Hope you ate your Wheaties this morning!" the guard chuckled.

"Wheaties?" asked Mulally.

"Yeah, the breakfast of champions!" laughed the guard.

First they stopped at the Liberty and Justice for All exhibit. "Here we are," said the guard. "This exhibit will take your breath away! It's about the struggle for freedom and the courage that it takes to keep it. It shows a new legacy of freedom for the future. All the symbolic artifacts are woven together with real folks' personal stories, and the villains and heroes too, as it balances progress and defines the meaning of American freedom. Lincoln's chair, Rosa Parks' bus, George Washington's camp chest are all part of our memory, representing not only historical events but attempting to personify the struggle. The Revolution really comes to life here. This exhibit celebrates the people who came before us, who had the resolve to think about and fight for our independence.

"Now look what we have here: the actual camp bed that General George Washington slept on at Valley Forge. What do you think?" grinned the guard, elbowing Mulally. "Maybe I should make a sign and put it up right there next to it that says 'Washington Slept Here.'"

"Yes," chuckled Mulally. "The tourists would sure get a kick out of that! They could stop in front of it and have their pictures taken." The two men laughed and continued down the museum hallway.

"Social and economic conditions past and present, weigh heavy on the American consciousness. Slavery had both moral and economic dimensions," explained the guard. "Harriett Beecher Stowe and Fredrick Douglass both pressed hard for emancipation that was not settled when the war broke out. Lincoln redefined what it meant to be an American and a human being."

Mulally nodded as they arrived at the Lincoln's Chair exhibit. "Isn't it incredible that the actual theatre chair where Lincoln was assassinated has been preserved for generations?" said Mulally.

"That's part of what preserving legacy is all about, son. Lincoln was loved and hated by many. Imagine being persecuted to vote?" the guard remarked. "Think about it. Would you allow yourself to be jailed for a cause?" asked the guard.

"I've often asked myself that question. I believe I would, if I felt that my voice and sacrifice was truly making a real difference," Mulally reflected.

"Would you die for a cause? Like idealistic young soldiers who give their lives for the cause of freedom, often not understanding why," asked the guard. "I've asked myself that question too. Don't mean to slobber philosophy all over you. Come on now, there is more to see, and I've got to get to my chores of cleaning up that new exhibition vehicle," said the guard.

They viewed the Independence timeline, which ran from 1618 to 1791, a painted image that showed George Washington in full length, standing on a cloud with the capitol building behind him and Mount Vernon and the Washington Tomb in opposite lower corners. The timeline reminded readers that while Independence was declared in 1776, it was fought for until 1791.

Mulally read from a letter that was in a glass enclosed case, from George Washington to Major General Israel Putnam (1718-1790). Wherein Washington writes, "You will not delay a moment in sending the Troops which are ordered. Their aid becomes more and more necessary."

"That's great leadership for you, fearless and relentless! General Washington didn't waste a moment in sending aid when needed," Mulally remarked.

"Timing is crucial in effective decision making," the guard smiled.

Then they came upon the artifact of the Declaration of Independence. The museum sign read: 'As the generation of the Revolution passed from memory, Congress authorized the printing of 200 exact copies of the Declaration. Only about 30 of these survive today.' Mulally then stood before the United States Constitution and recited the preamble out loud as the security guard listened on.

"We the people of the United States of America..."

They passed by the Freedom and Union Timeline, the Votes for Women, the Civil Rights Movement, and the Patriot Act. They moved down the hallway, around the bend and to the right, the cleaning bucket hanging on the security guard's arm, swinging and clanging; they walked until they reached the Made in America exhibit.

"Manufacturing and Power are the two sections of this exhibit that explore the legacy of American innovators from the 18th to 20th century that made America a manufacturing superpower. There are hundreds of artifacts, including operating steam engines," commented the guard.

They walked down yet another hallway to the Transportation and Mobility exhibit where the development of transportation before gas-powered vehicles was explored.

"And here we are in front of one of my all time favorite exhibits" exclaimed the security guard. "Automobiles in American Society."

"Mine too!" exclaimed Mulally with equal excitement.

"The automobile refashioned our nation's way of life more than any invention in history," said the guard.

"Sure has," said Mulally.

"Hey, check this out," said Mulally, rushing over to the 15 millionth Ford Model T Touring Car. Do you realize that this was the last car of the Model 'T' series?" shouted Mulally back over to the guard.

"Sure do! After completing this car, Ford began preparations to build the new model 'A'. The 4-cylinder, 22.5hp, five-passenger touring car is marked with Engine No. 15,000,000," the guard yelled back. They were as excited as two kids in a candy store.

"Here's the Tucker '48 automobile, brainchild of Preston Thomas Tucker and designed by renowned stylist, Alex Tremulis. This car represents one of the latest attempts by an independent car maker to break into the high-volume car business. Preston Tucker was one of the most recognized figures of the late 1940's, as controversial and enigmatic as his namesake automobile," the guard explained.

"Yes, but didn't it fail before it had a chance to succeed?" asked Mulally.

"It certainly did. Sometimes we learn more from our failures, than our successes," added the guard.

"Tell me more," said Mulally.

"We have nine battery powered cars, one battery powered truck, two solar powered cars and that's a total of twelve electric vehicles from 1896 to 1997! Remarkable, huh!" exclaimed the guard.

Stopping in front of the Ford Mustang #1, Mulally walked around the car as if having discovered it for the first time.

"Quite a piece of history this is. Imagine — the first Mustang ever produced!" Mulally exclaimed. "Sold in 1964, but it's really a 1965 model. This incredible vehicle fueled the 'pony craze' of the 1960's. It was also the first automobile to win the Tiffany Award for Excellence in American Design. What a car!"

They continued on past the McDonald's sign, one exhibit after the other and past by the Wright Flyer Replica and The Spirit of St. Louis. As they came upon the airplanes, Mulally paused and smiled.

"There's so much more here to see," said the guard.

Mulally noticed how the guard kept his distance — he wasn't an 'in your face' kind of guy. His security cap was serendipitously tipped down slightly over his eyebrows, revealing a kind and friendly smile. But the security guard didn't seem to take much for granted; his childlike enthusiasm and energy was contagious, as if he was visiting the museum for the very first time.

"By the way, what's your name?" Mulally asked the guard.

"Call me Joe. I'm just an average Joe," the man chuckled.

"Ok, Joe, where to next?" Mulally smiled.

"Follow me," Joe the security guard replied, tugging on his arm and pulling him in a new direction.

"I used to work for Ford, too," said Joe.

"Really? What did you do with the company," asked Mulally. Before Joe could respond, he continued. "It's really amazing just how many people you meet in America and from all walks of life who work directly or indirectly for the automobile industry."

The guard nodded and walked on ahead. They continued down a long darkened hallway that was suddenly getting uncomfortably warm, like the heat was turned up full blast. They passed by a closed door that had a sign on it which said 'Reflections of Man' exhibit. Steam seeped out from underneath the large steel door. Mulally tapped the guard on his shoulder.

"Hey, is that smoke coming out of that room?"

"It's part of the exhibit," replied Joe.

"Can I duck my head in there?" asked Mulally curiously.

"Sure. Every museum has an exhibit like this, but some people can see it and others can't," Joe replied.

"What does that mean?" said Mulally.

The guard didn't answer him. And then all of a sudden, the large steel door opened by itself and hot smoky steam poured out. "Head on in, son, if you like. It's quite a show. We still have some time. It's worth seeing. I think you can handle it," he smiled, "I'll be waiting for you here, right outside the door," the guard reassured him as he placed his cleaning bucket down on the floor and leaned against the wall.

Anxiousness, excitement — a multitude of emotions — filled every molecule of Mulally's being. Having a curious, adventurous nature and a built in GPS system that instinctively knew where he was heading, Mulally decided to go in. The steel door slammed shut behind him like a tomb.

The room was sweltering. Mulally removed his sport coat, folding it over his arm before he wiped the sweat from his forehead. He loosened his tie. In the center of the room was a stage-like exhibit platform. Hot white steam was rising up from underneath the platform, making it almost impossible to see anything in the room. Mulally walked around the platform, using the edges as a guide.

As the steam began to clear, he noticed a figure of a tall thin man with a pasty white complexion, in a pinstripe business suit and fedora hat, standing in the center of the stage. The man was holding a briefcase and a newspaper was tucked under his arm. Next to the man was a tall oval dressing room style mirror with a laser spotlight beaming down on him.

"Welcome to the Reflection of Man exhibit, the chronicles of human failure and doom," the man said, politely tipping his hat to Mulally. "This exhibit showcases a collection of man's broken dreams, stupidity and self-destruction. I started the collection when you were just an apple in your father's eye," he offered, boasting a wide maniacal grin.

"Come and see the cancer of your world, witness the utterly destructive forces of evil since the beginning of time," said the man. "See for yourself the other side of the human coin, as you celebrate the values of goodness and innovation. And then you decide."

There was a sign with an arrow which said *This Way Up,* pointing to steps to walk up onto the stage.

"Who are you?" Mulally called out.

"You, me, everybody. I'm called all kinds of names — snake oil salesman, crook, crony, shyster, bully, criminal, evil, and many variations of the same theme — imagine, some folk even call me the devil, but you don't see any horns and a tail, do you?" laughed the man, removing his hat. "If you're looking for answers, you've come to the right place."

The pounding of a drum, like the sound of a human heart beating could be heard in the distance. "Step right up and look in the mirror. Take a walk on the other side and see the real story of man through the looking glass of truth. Perhaps afterwards you'll remove your rose colored glasses and scrap your delusional optimism," he smiled.

It's probably the most recent hologram technology, thought Mulally.

"Step right up to the platform, sir," beckoned the man. "Come on now, you're not afraid are you?" he said tauntingly.

"I'm not afraid," Mulally smiled. Then he walked up the steps and onto the exhibit platform. The man pointed to the tall oval mirror next to him.

"Go ahead. Look at the man in the mirror. The show's about to begin," the man laughed.

Mulally turned, faced the mirror and looked inside, expecting to see his reflection. Instead, he stared into a dark, black hole. Then, suddenly, a virtual movie unfolded within it, beginning with the sounds and sights of war and destruction, natural and man-made disasters, murder, famine, massacres and man's conquests, from the beginning of time, for gold, God and glory. Horrific scenes reflected, played back at warp speed, one after the other beginning with the murder of Abel by his brother Cain, through a biblical and historical timeline scanning human history: Sodom and Gomorrah, Pharaoh's persecution of the Jews and the Christians by the Romans, the crucifixion of Jesus Christ, Mongol conquests and the Spanish Inquisition, the Great Proletarian Cultural Revolution in China and the Crusades, brother against brother in the bloody American Civil War, the massacres of the native people, slavery and suffrage. The images moved forward in time into the concentration camps of WWII, the Soviet purges under Stalin and the banning of religion and God, the bombing of Hiroshima, the POW camps in Vietnam, ethnic cleansing and genocide, a dying African continent, more wars, more hunger, more destruction, the greed and opulence of dictators, of industrialists and politicians, of Wall Street scammers and the golden palaces built through exploitation. Finally slowed down to a reflection of the 9/11 attack, replete with applauds by extremists as the towers fell, and then the aftermath, the senseless and tragic loss of human life.

Mulally watched in silence as the dark side of humanity was reflected and revealed. And with that last scene, the mirror went blank and then his reflection appeared. He stared at himself in the mirror for a few moments.

"Bravo, bravo, encore," the man in the pinstripe suit laughed joyfully, anticipating a victory.

Mulally turned around, faced the man, and glared back at him.

"Now, don't blame me," cowered the man. "That's your own reflection in the mirror, not mine. Man is a product of bad engineering, built with major defects, a dangerous and defective creation. Hopefully one day, as practice makes perfect, man will engineer a way to destroy the force that made this pathetic invention."

"You mean God," replied Mulally.

At the uttering of the word God, the man put his hands to his ears, seemingly to be in pain from hearing that word, but regained his composure and continued.

"Your prayers, hopes and dreams are an illusion. They cannot be heard by a deaf inventor. Man is the serial killer of humanity. You've come here to witness and celebrate achievements? Hah! Your automobile couldn't hold a candle against the pathological evil nature and destructive inventions of man."

Mulally closed his eyes and searched within. The images of destruction rocked his very being. He visualized all those brave and heroic people at Ground Zero. Those poor souls that jumped from the World Trade Center towers, trying to escape the burning inferno inside. He visualized strangers embracing each other, united as one, praying together on their final journey home.

Through the debris, he recalled seeing a random flowering weed and a single blade of grass breaking through the ground, reaching up to the sunlight. He recalled the blackened faces of the tireless rescue workers and the miraculous stories of faith and sacrifice. In the distance he saw a parade of trucks rolling in at Ground Zero, as the Detroit Three American automakers, Ford, Chrysler and GM, immediately came to the aid of their fallen economy, just as the Allied Armada disgorged their troops at five beaches along France's Normandy coast, ultimately leading to the Nazi defeat in the West. He noted that it was the American automobile companies, the true patriots, and thought how they didn't wait for legislative orders from an automotive Czar or appointed government bureaucrats. The Detroit Three marched on their own free will to roll up their sleeves to help save the American Dream.

Mulally saw himself as a little boy, running into the kitchen, thirsty after a long bike ride, his mother waiting for him, smiling and holding a glass of water. And as he drank it down, he heard his Mom say, 'remember Alan, the glass is always half full, not half empty.'

Mulally turned to the man and smiled.

"Thank you. It always helps to keep things in perspective," he said.

The master of ceremonies seemed pleased.

"So then, you agree with me? Man is a virus, the cancer of the world and all this celebration of innovation and ingenuity is hog wash?" he replied, wringing his hands together.

"No, on the contrary," said Mulally. "Here is the lesson. It's all about listening. We can choose to listen to the constructive voices or destructive voices within us and in our world. This reflective show serves to remind us about how precious life and liberty are and our obligation to safeguard them and to be grateful for what we have been given, far more than we deserve in most cases.

"There's no case of over-engineering when it comes to man. We're just the right balance and have the right number of parts. We're not robots. We have free will. It's all about accountability and making the right choices, don't you get it?" Mulally asked.

The spotlight on the stage dimmed and the man faded away. Lights turned on as the steel door opened wide; the show had ended. Mulally walked out of the Reflection of Man exhibit.

"Wow!" Mulally exclaimed, wiping off his brow. "What an exhibit! It seemed so real. So much human pain and suffering, yet such a will to survive and create, innovate, build and evolve — the inexhaustible efforts of ordinary men and women, whose tenacity has influenced the world to make it a better place. Our individual challenge is to have the courage to keep making the right choices every day despite difficulties — to turn obstacles into opportunities."

"Who we are is defined by who we strive to be. We're living the dream, son, living the dream," smiled the guard.

"It was literally as hot as hell in there," he said to the guard as he put his sport coat back on.

"Couldn't describe it better myself," the guard replied, and they continued down the hallway.

"We're about done with our tour, son, but there's one more thing I'd like to show you —saved the best for last," the guard announced, as they came to a halt in front of another exhibit which Mulally had never seen before at the Henry Ford Museum.

"Behold, the original built-to-order American-LaFrance Combination Chemical and Hose Car," he exclaimed with a newborn father's pride. Mulally walked all around it, awe struck by the ingenuity of its unique design and structure.

"This is incredible! Is this the first fire engine? I didn't think the original still existed?" he gasped.

"Sure is the real McCoy — on loan from George Washington's Mount Vernon — a personal favor to the boss," he smiled. "It was built in the 1920's. Back in those days, fire was a deadly enemy and a serious threat. This here is a special chemical fire truck, blending the modern firefighting weapons and techniques of its time, combining the dependability of a Ford vehicle, resulting in the ultimate in historic fire protection. The General surely appreciated it. You know, son, it's because of this fire truck that the Henry Ford Museum came about. Those incredible women at Mount Vernon Ladies Association were tireless in their effort to preserve and protect the memory of George Washington and the heritage of Mount Vernon; they provided the inspiration for this museum."

The guard removed the rags from his bucket and a plastic spray bottle and started to wipe clean and shine the side of the fire truck.

"Hey, how about giving me a hand here?" he asked, taking out another rag and spray bottle from the bucket and handing it to Mulally.

Without hesitation, Mulally went right to work cleaning the fire truck.

"You take the right side and I'll get the left and we'll meet at the back. Why, together and in no time, we'll have this vehicle looking brand new," the guard said excitedly.

"Can you imagine," called Mulally to the guard, "that this incredible fire engine was state of the art in its day?"

"Sure was," the guard yelled back.

And as they continued to shine it, the truck came back to life.

"The guys back at headquarters should see me now," barked Mulally as he polished the hood of the engine. "Boy, this hood is really hot. Seems like the engine's been running."

Then he climbed up and hopped into the driver's seat. There was a fire hat on the seat next to him. He put it on his head and looked at himself in the rear view mirror and smiled.

From the corner of his eye, he noticed a white parchment envelope on the floor of the passenger side. He picked it up. It was addressed to Christopher Hope and had a broken official wax seal. It bore the scripted initials of GW, Mount Vernon. Mulally placed the envelope in his coat pocket and smiled. The security guard was calling to him.

"I've got to go now, son. It's about opening time now. Your meeting is about to start in the conference room," he yelled from behind the fire truck.

Mulally jumped down from the truck and circled it, looking for Joe, but he was already gone. He wasn't sure what meeting the security guard was referring to, since the museum was about to open.

The conference room door was ajar; Mulally walked inside. Two chairs faced each other in the center of the empty room. He noticed an object on one of the chairs, walked over and found Joe's security hat on the seat. He picked it up and looked around and then sat down and placed the hat on his lap. He glanced down at his watch, and then up at the wall clock above the conference room door. The hour hand was positioned on seven.

From a distance, he could hear the echo of tapping footsteps on the stone floor as someone was approaching from down the hallway. The pace was brisk, getting closer, the footsteps louder and louder. Adrenalin shot through him and his heart raced. In walked a man he could never forget, a man wearing a black derby hat, elegantly dressed in a cream colored three-piece suit, smiling and looking robust and happy. Overcome with emotion, Mulally got up to greet him.

"Alan!" exclaimed Mr. Carman, offering a robust handshake and patting him on the back.

"Why, you look great," beamed Mulally, overcome with emotion.

"Thank you! I've never felt better. You keep up the great work and doing the right things, and I may just get out on the golf course before you know it," he smiled. "You know what Will Rogers said, 'I guess there is nothing that will get your mind off everything like golf.' I have never been depressed enough to take up the game, but they say you get so sore at yourself you forget about everything else."

Mr. Carman glanced curiously at the hat in Mulally's hand.

"Belongs to a friend of mine," smiled Mulally.

Mr. Carman nodded. "Please, sit down. You wanted to see me?" He spoke in a more serious tone.

"Yes, sir," said Mulally.

"Why don't you go ahead and close the door? Let's you and I talk." replied Mr. Carman. Mulally closed the conference room door and the two leaders had their meeting. After a while, the conference room door opened and Mulally walked out alone. The museum was now open, and people were streaming in.

"What time did you get here? Is your phone off?" Mulally's assistant asked.

"I wanted to get here a little early today to fill up the tank with inspiration, go over important issues and get some clarity. And I sure did," he smiled.

His assistant walked over to the conference room and hung the press conference sign, then walked inside with the press kits.

"What's that?" asked his assistant pointing to the hat in his hands.

"Oh, this? It belongs to a friend of mine — Joe, the security guard. I'll be right back."

Mulally walked down to the security station.

"Joe forgot his hat," he smiled at the receptionist.

"Joe? There's no Joe working security here, sir," she replied.

"Hmm, I didn't think so," Mulally smiled. "Well, here's his hat anyway. Keep it for him in case he comes back, will you?" he asked.

The day's events unfolded as a moving tribute to the founder of Ford Motor Company, and a celebration reminding America of what it truly meant to be an American. Positive energy from the history, exhibits, stories, ideas, and good news could have lit up the world.

It was nearing closing time when Mulally and Christopher met up in the lobby. "What a wonderful day this was! How do you think our message was received by everyone?" asked Mulally.

"If we could bottle up your message and what happened here today, and send it to every single person, just imagine!" exclaimed Christopher.

"I want to thank you and your team for making this day the incredible success it was," smiled Mulally. "Free for lunch tomorrow?"

"Sure," replied Christopher.

"How about Fairlane Manor?" he winked.

"I'd like that," he replied.

"I'll drive. The weather's been unusually clear all week. Um… as a matter of fact, I was at Fairlane just a few days ago — went there for some fresh ideas and inspiration," explained Christopher.

"I figured you had been," Mulally replied. Reaching into his pocket, he removed the envelope he found in the fire truck. "Oh, by the way, I think this belongs to you," he said, handing over the envelope addressed to Christopher from GW.

"Thanks, but actually, what's inside of it is yours," he replied, removing from the envelope the letter addressed to Alan Mulally from GW and handing it to him. I was asked to give it to you. I must have misplaced it. Where did you find it?" asked Christopher.

"While Joe and I were polishing up the fire engine, you know, the original one that Ford made especially for Mount Vernon? I found this envelope lying on the floor of the passenger seat. Your name was on it so I figured I'd give it to you at the end of the day," Mulally explained.

"Joe?" asked Christopher.

"Yeah, a real friendly fellow. Had a real jump in his step. He sure gave me a run for my money. I got a personal tour of the museum this morning, and saw the fire engine that was brought in today on loan from Mount Vernon. The vehicle had some work done on the motor yesterday, so Joe and I cleaned and shined it all up. Seemed to have been on the road lately. The engine was real hot," Mulally explained.

"I see," smiled Christopher. "Where is that fire engine now?" asked Christopher.

"It's just around the bend," said Mulally. "Come on, follow me." Mulally sped on ahead of Christopher, who despite taking giant steps, could barely keep up with him as they hurried back down the hallway. The museum lights flickered. Turning the corner, they stopped in front of a large empty exhibition space.

"It's gone now," said Mulally disappointedly. "It must have been returned to where it came from."

"Probably was. I guess the envelope must have fallen out of my jacket pocket," Christopher grinned.

"Guess it must have," Mulally grinned back. "I'll see you then tomorrow morning in the lobby, at, let's say 11 a.m., if that works for you," said Mulally.

"Thanks, see you then," smiled Christopher.

Mulally was the first to visit the Ford Museum that morning, and he was also the last to leave. Before exiting, he sat on the edge of a long marble bench in the lobby for a few moments. Reaching into his coat pocket, he gently removed the envelope addressed to him from GW. Alone, with a slight tremor of hand, and in the silence of the grand hallways of history, he read:

Mount Vernon
Alexandria, Virginia
GW

Mount Vernon - 6 April

Mr. Alan Mulally

Sir,

    It is the actions, and not the commission that makes the officer, and that there is more expected from him, than the title. Your actions define you — trust in God and give each other encouragement — and always be honest.

    In this effort, leader to leader, allow me to share with you, sir, an excerpt of a correspondence I had written on July 2, 1776 — the height of the Revolutionary War, in my efforts to reinforce my officers and soldiers where their focus should be in our struggle for independence against the British. I stress the importance of humility, code of conduct, hard work and team work and reliance upon the Lord's providence.

    "Our own Country's Honor, all call upon us for a vigorous and manly exertion, and if we now shamefully fail, we shall become infamous to the whole world. Let us therefore rely upon the goodness of the Cause, and the aid of the supreme Being, in whose hands Victory is, to animate and encourage us to great and noble Actions — The Eyes of all our Countrymen are now upon us, and we shall have their blessings, and praises, if happily we are the instruments of saving them from the Tyranny mediated against them. Let us therefore animate and encourage each other, and show the whole world, that a free man contending for Liberty on his own ground is superior to any slavish mercenary on earth."

G Washington

Mulally placed the letter back into his coat pocket and smiled. He would treasure it forever. Who could ever imagine such a gift? How blessed and grateful he was. He had one last thing to do, one last issue of the day to resolve. As the museum staff hurried about, closing up for the evening, Mulally headed in the direction of the 'Reflections of Man' exhibit.

Turning the corner where he and Joe had been earlier in the morning, he was certain he was standing at the exact spot where the large steel door with the steam coming out had been. But there was no door, no room, no exhibit, only a bronze plaque on a museum wall with a quote inscribed:

> *'Into the hands of every individual is given a marvelous power for good or evil — the silent, unconscious, unseen influence of his life. This is simply the constant radiation of what man really is, not what he pretends to be.'* — *William George Jordan*

Mulally reflected for a moment, let out a deep sigh, and headed towards the exit. The lights went out at the museum. Another extraordinary day had come to an end, and another one was on the horizon.

The very next morning, Alan and Christopher met at the Ford office as planned, then headed out for lunch together at Fairlane Manor. Just as Mulally had predicted, it was a picture perfect day. They left early for their noontime reservation, allowing plenty of time to talk.

On the way, they shared the events of the last few days, reviewing the challenges facing the company and the country, and the opportunities those challenges afforded. Christopher was grateful to have time alone with Alan Mulally. He was an ordinary guy, but an extraordinary leader. Christopher thought to himself, *if you're fortunate enough to be in the presence of true greatness just one time in your life — you're truly blessed.*

"You're a steadfast optimist with a positive outlook on things even in the most challenging situations," said Christopher to Mulally, on their drive to Fairlane. Mulally smiled.

"I got that gift from my Mom. She always sees the glass half full, rather than half empty. But, Henry Ford was the ultimate optimist. He said that 'Whether you think you can, or you can't, you are usually right!' He also said that, 'There is no happiness except in the realization that we have accomplished something, and that 'failure is only the opportunity to begin again more intelligently.'"

"Henry Ford was a genius, yet he made common sense common practice," Christopher replied.

"He certainly did," responded Mulally.

When they pulled into the crowded parking lot at Fairlane Manor, Mulally's eyes seem to water a bit and Christopher looked the other way, also fighting back the overpowering emotions inside. Crowds of visitors milled about the manor ground. On the porch were several empty rocking chairs lined up in a row. Approaching the entrance, Mulally turned to Christopher.

"You want to rock a bit... for old time's sake?" he winked.

"Yeah, let's rock!" Christopher grinned, and the two men rushed over to the rockers like youngsters playing musical chairs. Oblivious to the folks coming and going, they gently rocked in nostalgic bliss to the memories of their visits to the manor and the meetings with Mr. Carman. Soon, it was time for their lunch reservation.

"Welcome Mr. Mulally, Mr. Hope," smiled the hostess. "Your table is ready, please follow me."

"Did you check the time on the grandfather clock?" smiled Christopher.

"No. What's the point? We both know what time it is," Mulally smiled back.

As they followed the hostess to their table, they noticed someone waving at them from in the middle of the restaurant. The hostess guided them right to that table and as they got closer, they immediately recognized who it was.

"I thought I might find you two here," smiled Mr. Carman, getting up from his seat and reaching out his hand. The table was set for three.

"Our lunch is ordered and some nice hot soybean tea is on the way, gentlemen," said Mr. Carman.

Christopher tried hard to contain his reaction when he noticed that both Mr. Carman and Alan Mulally were wearing a similar colored red tie.

"Alan," said Mr. Carman in an upbeat tone, "first off, I want you to tell my great-grandson, Bill, all the family and the leadership team, that they are doing a wonderful job. Please remind them that our mission is much greater than returning Ford to the greatness we once enjoyed. The task is also to restore and preserve the American Dream. Each one of you is not only entrusted to protect the Ford legacy, but the American Dream too."

Albert arrived with a silver tray, three cups of tea, and several plates of food. The dining room was bustling with activity and loud conversation. Mulally leaned closer to Mr. Carman, making certain that he heard every single word.

"As we reflect over this past week, I've been reminded of the struggles we faced in the birth and development as a nation," explained Mr. Carman. "Ford has always been there for America. When America needed us to shut down the assembly plants to make war planes, we did it. When America needed us to make tanks, we shut down all the automobile operations and made only military equipment. Ford was always able to continue because we were strong and could come to America's aid, just like Americans have always been there for Ford. We worked together to build a great country and a great company. That's the legacy I've always wanted — a great America as well as a great company. Ford made up the difference when America needed funding for national monuments. We helped open hospitals and provided funding for colleges and universities. We have literally provided billions of dollars for American interests. It's never been just about making great vehicles to sell, but continuing our legacy of making the world a better place to live.

"Later on in my life, I began to read more and learn more about history and many other things. Did you know that the Founders of our nation, although from diverse backgrounds, all had one thing in common — they were well-read men? The foundation and principles of our Constitution are based on that common bond of knowledge. Martin Luther King came back to tell us to adjust the vision — true diversity is treating people equally and having common principles and a common dream. Knowledge is power. We should focus more on what we have in common than on what makes us different. Although we can't go back and erase the mistakes of the past, we can press forward and build a mountain of achievements. I've always said that we learn more from our failures than from our successes.

"My main focus, as you know," explained Mr. Carman, "was to bring transportation to the masses so that people would have a better life. We've passed through difficult times before — through the Revolutionary War, the War of 1812, the Civil War and the Alamo. Although the Alamo fell in the early morning hours of March 6, 1836, the death of the Alamo defenders symbolizes courage and sacrifice for the cause of liberty. Then we had the World Wars, and other conflicts almost continually — at home and overseas. We had the Great Depression. That's why it's referred to as the 'Great Depression.' Through the sufferings of the Depression, 'great' things came out of it. Ford was shaped during the Depression and aspects of that thrive until this very day.

"You're holding the reins now, Alan. Use your options and choices wisely and call upon your faith for strength, courage and guidance. Your challenge is to keep Ford strong. Remember to remind Americans what made America great.

"Alan, please tell Bill, Edsel, and the rest of my family, that I'm very proud they are continuing my legacy and of the true leadership they've shown. The family has made the right choices by standing tall with you, your vision and your plan. Your accomplishments while at Ford have been exemplary; I knew when I first met you that you were up to the call."

Mr. Carman continued, "Alan, always remember, what makes America great are the people. Albert Einstein once said, 'Not everything that can be counted counts, and not everything that counts can be counted.' Please remember all that we've talked about. I'll be checking in on you and the team from time to time."

"Thank you sir, said Mulally. I promise we will do everything in our power to continue to make you and America very proud."

Mr. Carman smiled.

"Life isn't about how we survive the storm,
it's how we dance in the rain." — Mr. Carman

PRESS RELEASE

The Memorial of Founder Henry Ford Marks a Tribute to America and Provides Lessons in Leading in Difficult Times

A Strong Ford = A Strong America = A Strong World

For Immediate Release: DEARBORN, Mich., April 7 — Ford Motor Company announced today the annual memorial message about Henry Ford, founder of Ford Motor Company. This memorial marks a Tribute to America and provides lessons of leadership during challenging times.

According to Ford's Vice-President of Public Relations, Christopher Hope, "Ford Motor Company is implementing The Ford One Team Restructuring Plan. As a result, Ford was able to refuse a government bailout offered to the automotive industry. Ford has been working to turn around the company with exciting new products and renewed energy from its dealers and employees. Ford is once again on the road to greatness — all of this, in the midst of an economic and political crisis facing America and the world."

This year's anniversary message focuses on a 'Tribute to America' and provides leadership lessons during challenging times. The company organized an anniversary event at the Henry Ford Museum, where Ford's leaders and employees paid tribute to Time magazines' 'Man of the Century,' Henry Ford. The exhibits and events showcased America's ingenuity and innovation throughout its history and the generosity and continual support by the Ford family throughout the generations, to preserve our American history and continue the legacy.

According to Ford's President and CEO, Alan Mulally, "Our mission is to keep Ford strong and remind Americans what made America great. We've gone through challenging times before and thrived. We will do so again. Great things come out of great difficulties. You can thrive and grow your business if you do the right things. Henry Ford reminds us that, 'If you do the right thing, at the right time, with the right motivation, you will get the right results. But even more importantly, you will earn the right to expect others to do the same.' The American Dream is represented by our hard work to create a better world for future generations. There are no guarantees, but there is always opportunity through hard work and living the American Dream. The secret to great leadership lies in the ability to make decisions today, that improve the lives of people tomorrow."

According to Ford Motor Company's founder, Henry Ford, "We are in partnership with America. We were always able to survive because Ford was strong and could come to America's aid, just like Americans have always supported Ford. We worked together to build a great America and a great company. Coming together is a beginning, staying together is progress, and working together is success. Failure is only the opportunity to begin again more intelligently, and whether you think that you can, or that you can't, you're usually right. It isn't just about making great vehicles, it's about continuing the legacy in improving the lives of people and making the world a better place to live."

Source: Driving the American Dream Team Public Relations

HENRY FORD WAS famous for founding Ford Motor Company, but the positive impact his life had on society reaches far beyond the automotive industry. Henry Ford changed America through the simple genius upon which he founded his company. As the first to pay minorities and women equal pay for equal work, he was the ultimate defender of human rights with a vision to improve the quality of life for the common man. When the going wage was $2.50 a day, Ford paid $5.00 a day so his workers could afford the product they were building.

Ford's Model T was the chief instrument leading to one of the greatest and most rapid changes in the lives of common people in modern history. The original Ford cars were made for and by everyday Americans. Ford factories provided jobs that paid a living wage, leading to the evolution of the middle class in America. The Model T relieved rural farmers of isolation.

Eventually, the invention of the automobile and its accessibility to the majority of Americans allowed cities to spread outward, creating suburbs and housing developments. Where previous generations rarely ventured more than 15 miles from their birthplace, the affordable automobile opened up the entire country to them. Henry Ford's vision transitioned American society from the agricultural era into the industrial era.

FORD MOTOR COMPANY, a global automotive industry leader based in Dearborn, Mich., manufactures and distributes automobiles across six continents. With about 205,000 employees and about 90 plants worldwide, the company's automotive brands include Ford, Lincoln, Mercury and Volvo. The company provides financial services through Ford Motor Credit Company. For more information regarding Ford's products, please visit www.ford.com.

For more information, visit our website at:
www.thereturntogreatness.com

CLIFTON PETER LAMBRETH

CLIFTON PETER LAMBRETH has worked for the Ford Motor Company for over 25 years in a variety of positions. He has been a rainmaker at every position he has held. He has consistently been a top performer throughout his career at Ford having received prestigious awards and distinctions including five Ford Inuksuk Drive for Leaders Awards. He has also won three Diversity Leadership awards. Mr. Lambreth was one of a very few people at Ford worldwide to receive the 2008 Ford Leadership Award.

Clifton was a Ford college recruiter for over 10 years at Cornell University, University of Pennsylvania, Johnson Business School and Wharton Business School. He graduated from Thomasville Senior High School in North Carolina having been a proud alumnus of the North Carolina Baptist Children's Mills Home. He went on to receive his BSBA in Marketing and Management and his MBA from Western Carolina University.

He serves on the Board of Directors of the Family Foundation Fund, on the Executive Advisory Board of Lead like Jesus Foundation, Western Carolina's Alumni Board and on the Advisory Board for Western Carolina University's School of Business.

He is CEO of Daniel Bradley Matthews, Inc., providers of strategic automotive, business and marketing consulting. Mr. Lambreth also serves as an adviser to six different private businesses.

He was the associate producer of the weekly RFD TV show "Music and Motors" for 3 seasons.

As a sought-after business, marketing and automotive industry sector specialist, television personality and published author, Clifton Lambreth has authored and published various main media articles on diversity, compensation, leadership issues and other such hot topics. He has been quoted in over 500 different media sources.

Clifton also tours the nation speaking to various business and community organizations. He was the star of a recent television show, *The CEO Café*. Mr. Lambreth has given speeches to over 100 groups on motivation and success principles. He has also conducted numerous radio show interviews. He has been on NBC, CBS, ABC and Fox TV discussing a variety of business topics.

His first book, *Ford and the American Dream: Founded on Right Decisions*, has been translated into Russian. A book tour is planned for Russia early in 2010. A movie inspired by the book is underway for 2010 as well.

He also enjoys running and racing, and has run the Marine Corps Marathon, Philadelphia Marathon and the Boston Marathon. He competed in over 200 different 5K /10K races. Clifton has three sons and lives with his wife Susan and family in Brentwood, Tennessee.

MARY HELEN CALIA

MARY HELEN CALIA is a published author of business novels, industry features, adult and teen fiction, and musical compositions and scores. Her professional career in business and international communications, investor and public relations spans more than twenty-five years. She is a co-author of the bestselling business novel, *Ford and the American Dream: Founded on Right Decisions* in addition to Great Leaders Listen; Results: Winning in Difficult Times; Legacy Living and other leadership books. She is the author of a new teen action book on school yard bullying, which has received kudos from the American Medical Association, Paulina Star.

Mary is a graduate of Grover Cleveland High School in Queens, New York, then continued her education City College of New York and Austin Peay State University in Tennessee. She began her professional career at the Hospital for Special Surgery in New York City, where she was awarded an honorable mention for her research assistance in total knee replacement as reported in the New England Journal of Bone and Joint Surgery.

She co-founded North America's first full-service and award winning investor relations firm with the legendary communications' innovator, Marcel Knecht of Marcel Knecht & Associates, Inc., servicing more than 500 pubic companies worldwide. Mary helped launch Europe's first investor relations firm in Paris, France, and produced the first nationally-televised investment conference in North America. Her clients include

Power Corporation of Canada, Alcan Aluminum, Elf Aquitaine, NASDAQ and others.

Mary provides counsel to government leaders, emerging growth companies, Fortune 500 CEO's and political, business, celebrity, arts, culture and industry leaders. In international relations, she has collaborated in trade and industry, commerce and cultural communications with world and business leaders in the public and private sector. She has been featured as one of America's top businesswomen in leading business journals including the Nashville Business Journal.

She has served on numerous boards including the Montreal Neurological Hospital and the Jewish General Hospital, and is a member of the IABC (International Association of Business Communicators) and the Women's Club of Nashville. She is a public speaker on ethics, transparency, and school yard bullying.

Mary has four sons and lives and works in both New York City and Brentwood, Tennessee.

PATRICK JOSEPH DOYLE

PATRICK JOSEPH DOYLE has worked for Ford Motor Company for over twenty-four years in a variety of different Sales and Marketing positions and locations throughout the country. He has thoroughly enjoyed his career with Ford and has consistently been a top performer in every assignment. He has been a recipient of many leadership awards along the way including the "Diversity and Work-life Summit" award that recognizes those employees who work to build a culture that values diversity and work-life integration at Ford. He has also been a multiple award winner of the "Drive For Leaders At All Levels" which is a recognition program that celebrates individuals who demonstrate leadership qualities that positively impact the personal and professional development of others. Pat used a two year break in service with Ford to learn the automotive retail business first hand as the Fixed Operations Director at Courtesy Ford in Denver, Colorado.

Pat graduated from Chippewa Hills High School in Remus, Michigan and went on to earn a Bachelor of Science degree in Marketing Sales from Ferris State University in Big Rapids, Michigan. He is a public speaker and author. He is also very involved with the Sportsmen's Legacy Foundation, where the mission is to help provide lasting, quality outdoor mentorship to children who have lost a parent as a result of public service. He enjoys sharing his passion for hunting and fishing with kids through youth programs at Gilbert Creek Ranch in Mecosta, Michigan and Timmons Ranch in Blackford, Kentucky. Pat is married and lives with his family in Franklin, Tennessee.

IGOR BABAILOV

IGOR BABAILOV, MFA, is one of the most sought-after artists of our time. Recipient of numerous awards, Babailov received his master of fine arts degree doctorate level from the prestigious Surikov Academy. His works are widely shown in museums, galleries, and private collections worldwide. He has painted officially commissioned portraits of world leaders, celebrities, and social, business, and political elite, including Pope Benedict XVI (Vatican Museum); Pope John Paul II (Vatican Museum); President George Washington (Mount Vernon Estate and Museum); President George W. Bush (Presidential Collection); President Nelson Mandela (Presidential Collection, South Africa); President Vladimir Putin of Russia (Presidential Collection/Kremlin); Prime Minister Brian Mulroney of Canada (House of Commons/Parliamentary Gallery); America's Mayor, Rudolph Giuliani (Giuliani Partners, NYC); Secretary of State and Former First Lady Hillary R. Clinton (Clinton Presidential Library); The Honorable Joseph P. Sullivan, Justice, Appellate Division of the Supreme Court of the State of New York; renowned pianist Byron Janis (Steinway Hall Museum, NYC); legendary filmmaker Akira Kurosawa (Starlight Starbright Foundation, Japan), Bob Costas (Joe DiMaggio Collection); Reggie Jackson, Tiki Barber, Boomer Esiason, Bobby Hull, James Gandolfini, Regis Philbin, and many others. New York Magazine featured Babailov as one of America's top artists of our times and he is acclaimed by critics and contemporaries as 'Living Master." He serves on several distinguished boards, including the Child Art Foundation in Washington, D.C. Babailov is a member of the prestigious National Arts Club in New York, recipient of the international arts award 2009 "The Golden Star" medal and order of "Serving the Arts 1st Degree." He is an exclusive speaker of the celebrated Harry Walker Speakers Agency of New York. See www.Babailov.com.